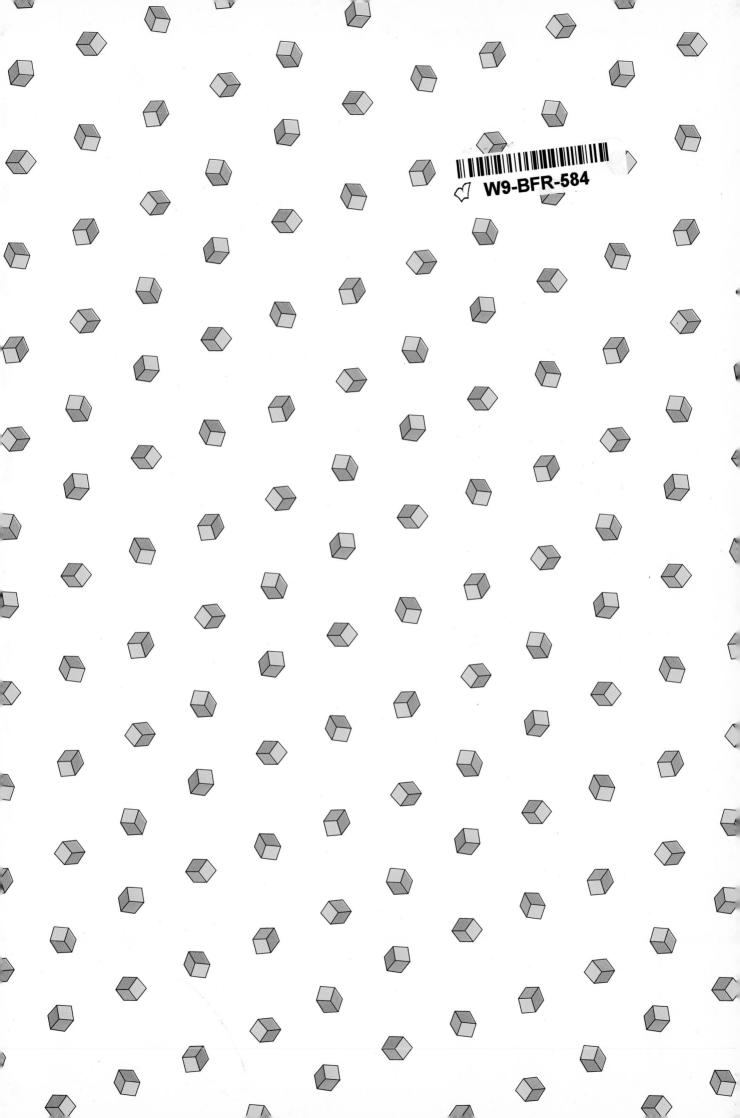

KNITS FOR KIDS

KNITS FOR KIDS

Lena Stengard

Macmillan Publishing Company
New York

Maxwell Macmillan International
New York Oxford Singapore Sydney

Acknowledgments

Many people devoted a lot of time and energy to ensure that this book was completed on time. Without Pamela Bell it would not have been possible, and I appreciate too the help I received from Sarah, Joan, Belinda, and Nina. Special thanks go to my husband, family, and friends for being so understanding throughout.

The following children were wonderful during our photographic sessions: Jack Boone, Elisabeth Harford, Arabella Benson, Milo Dickenson, Louise Harford, Chelsea Leyland, Antonia Hall, Jamie Scott, Octavia Dickenson, Jasmin Fisher, Louisa Fisher, Fabian Mander, Hal Messel, Julian Erleigh, Laura Proudlock, Oliver Proudlock, Ashley Connell, Claudia Legge, Edward Legge.

Patterns were written by Terri Cawthorn, and the checker was Janet Bentley.

The knitters who worked so hard were: Sue Mitchell, Audrey Clay, Alison Horton, Judy Baker, Doreen Ford, Audrey Whittaker, Sue Upton, Thelma German, Gwen Veale, Phyllis Haines. The beautiful locations featured in Gloucestershire were: Lasborough Park, Osleworth Park, Newark Park, Wortley House, Jaynes Court, Owlpen Manor.

Photographer Tracey Orme did a terrific job on location.

Many thanks to all the companies and individuals who helped me with clothes and accessories: Young England, for lending clothes to go with the designs, and Rosalind Mellor at the Great Western Antiques Center, Bath, for pretty Victorian accessories. Rowan Yarns were generous in supplying yarn for all the styles.

Finally, I'm very grateful to Eve Harlow and Elizabeth Nicholson, the editors, for putting everything together.

Young England, 47 Elizabeth Street, London SW1 W9PP. Tel: 071 259 9003
Buttons from: The Button Queen, 19 Marylebone Lane, London W1M 5FF. Tel: 071 935 1505
Pearls from: Ells and Farrier, 20 Princes Street, Hanover Square, London W1R 8PH. Tel: 071 629 9964

•

Macmillan Publishing Company
866 Third Avenue, New York, NY 10022

First published in Great Britain: in 1990 by Anaya Publishers Ltd, 49 Neal Street, London WC2H 9PJ

Editor for the US edition: Eleanor Van Zandt
Photography by Tracey Orme
Styling by Lena Stengard
Charts by Julie Ward
Technique Drawings by Coral Mula

Library of Congress Cataloging in Publication Data
Stengard, Lena
    Knits for kids/Lena Stengard
        p.   cm.
    "First published in Great Britain by Anaya Publishers . . . London" - Copr.p.

    ISBN 0-02-613951
        1. Knitting—Patterns   2. Children's clothing.   I. Title.
    TT825.S735 1991
    746.9'2—dc20   90-21465

                                                                        CIP

ISBN 0-02-613951-0

Macmillan books are available at special discounts for bulk purchases for sales promotions, premiums, fund-raising, or educational use. For details, contact:

Special Sales Director
Macmillan Publishing Company
866 Third Avenue
New York, NY 10022

10 9 8 7 6 5 4 3 2 1

Printed and bound in Great Britain by Clays Ltd, Bungay, Suffolk

Contents

Introduction

I WAS BORN IN Sweden, and from my earliest childhood was interested in dressing up. When I was six or seven I used to try on my grandmother's beautiful dresses. Before I left school I started modelling and used the money I earned to buy clothes and to start travelling. In 1967 I left Sweden for Milan, where I began a modelling career that took me to England, Germany, France, and Japan.

Later I moved to Devon, in England, and discovered rummage sales. I quickly built up a collection of clothes from the thirties and forties, which I sold to friends. This is how I met Edina Ronay. who was also collecting in a similar way. Together, she and I set up a stall in London selling antique clothes and lace. A year later we transferred from the stall to our own shop, and we found that our selection of hand-knitted sweaters from the thirties and forties were particularly popular. We therefore decided to expand this side of the business by having more pullovers knitted up from the original patterns.

I spent three days driving around Devon and built up a team of sixty talented hand-knitters who, a year and a half later, helped us to produce our third collection. This we showed in New York, Paris, and London, with such success that soon we were selling pullovers to department stores and boutiques all over the world. Our team of knitters had to be increased to one thousand to cope with the demand.

After five years my partnership with Edina Ronay dissolved and we went our separate ways. I stopped working for a while to have my third child and to spend more time with my family. When I returned to the world of knitwear design I spent two and a half years working with a team of two thousand knitters to produce collections for Laura Ashley, Mulberry, and Ralph Lauren, as well as my own Lena Stengard collection. This was all on a grander scale than anything I had done before, and although it was exciting, I found that the business had grown too big and was taking up all my waking hours, leaving me without enough time for my family. We decided to move to the Gloucestershire countryside, and I had my fourth child.

SOMETHING FOR EVERYONE

I was delighted when I was asked to put together a collection of children's knitwear for this book, since I have always loved to dress my own children in lovely clothes. Really good knitwear for the young is, however, difficult to find and always expensive, so I was particularly inspired by the idea of patterns to knit up oneself. I have tried to ensure that the selection includes something for knitters of all abilities, and something for the children to wear for all occasions, be it for parties, sports, or everyday wear. All the styles are classics which will not date, and if well looked after, they will last to be passed on and on. When designing for this book, I started with things I like to wear myself and then adapted them for children. As a result I think most of the styles in the book would look good on people of all ages from toddlers to grown-ups.

The book starts with simple classics that are easy for anyone to knit. Although these represent the basic essentials, they can be turned into something special with simple additions such as a tartan trim, a lace collar, or beautiful buttons. The pullovers on pages 10–25 are based on 1940s styles and are meant for special occasions. The designs in the cable section show what a variety of shapes and styles can be made from one simple cable stitch. The bobble collection may look difficult, but in fact these designs are as easy to knit as the cables. The Fair Isle designs are all adapted from traditional patterns, and they make timeless and ageless knits that look good on all the family. When I was a child in Sweden we all wore thick Scandinavian pullovers, especially for skiing, but these lovely pullovers are almost impossible to buy for children outside Scandinavia. I hope the patterns given here will mean that many more children in other countries will now be able to wear them. These Scandinavian pullovers and the ones that follow them in the book reflect the range of different national traditions that have influenced my designing. The Tyrolean group, for instance, was inspired by characteristic Austrian motifs. Having lived for twenty years in Britain, I have come to love all types of Scottish tartan, and have designed some hand-knitted tartan pullovers based on traditional colors.

STYLES IN SUMMER YARNS

Whenever I have felt that a design would be complemented by a hat or beret, or perhaps a baby's bonnet, I have included a pattern for this to create a complete outfit. I have also produced summer versions of many of the patterns, knitted up in light sunny colors and in cotton yarns.

After many years in the knitwear business I have developed a particular liking for the color range and quality of Rowan yarns, and I have used these throughout the book. The yarns are easily available from Rowan outlets worldwide, and specific information on retailers is given at the back of the book.

These patterns have given me great pleasure to design, and I very much hope that they will be satisfying to knit and that many children will enjoy wearing the finished results.

LENA STENGARD AT HOME WITH TWO OF HER CHILDREN, LAURA AND OLIVER

How to use this book

MEASUREMENTS

Before starting to knit it is essential to measure the child. Take the chest measurement about 5cm (2in) below the armpit and the sleeve seam from below the armpit to wrist.

The garments in this book are sized according to age, but this is only a guideline. If your two-year-old is a large child, you may want to knit a size larger. Check measurements carefully before beginning to knit, for adjustments may have to be made in the sleeve length or the length of the side seam. Most garments in this book are designed in three sizes: 6 months, 2 years, and 4 years. Once you decide on the size you are going to knit, keep to it throughout the pattern. The chart below gives approximate measurements for the three sizes, in centimeters and inches.

		6 mth		2 yr		4 yr	
Chest	cm	48		58.5		63.5	
	in	19		23		25	
Sleeve	cm	19		23		28	
	in	7$^{1}/_{2}$		9		11	
Overall length		Short	Long	Short	Long	Short	Long
	cm	25.5	30.5	31.5	37	35.5	40.5
	in	10	12	12$^{1}/_{2}$	14$^{1}/_{2}$	14	16

GAUGE

The required gauge is given at the beginning of every pattern. To produce a garment of the right size, you must obtain the correct gauge, which is given as the number of stitches and rows required to produce a 10cm (4in) square of knitting. People differ considerably in the amount of tension they exert on the yarn when knitting. This is why you must check the gauge you obtain against that obtained by the designer, and, if necessary, adjust the needle size.

To check the gauge, cast on a few more stitches than those specified, and work for a few more rows than specified (those at the edge are difficult to count), using the recommended size of needles.

Work the number of rows given. Bind off and press or block the square lightly. Using a ruler, measure and count the stitches and rows. If you have more stitches and rows than that recommended for the pattern, try again with larger size needles. If you have fewer stitches and rows, try again with smaller size needles.

It is worth taking time to ensure that your gauge is correct; otherwise an ill-fitting garment will result.

•

THE PATTERN FOR JAMIE'S COTTON DOUBLE-BREASTED CARDIGAN IS ON PAGE 100

NEEDLES

The chart shows knitting needle sizes in metric, American sizes. The chart shows the closest equivalent American needle size for each metric size. Bear in mind, however, tha these sizes are only approximate equivalents; so you should not mix metric and American needles in the same piece of knitting.

Continental mm												
2	2$^{1}/_{4}$	2$^{3}/_{4}$	3	3$^{1}/_{4}$	3$^{1}/_{2}$	3$^{3}/_{4}$	4	4$^{1}/_{2}$	5	5$^{1}/_{2}$	6	6$^{1}/_{2}$
American												
0	1	2	–	3	4	5	6	7	8	9	10	10$^{1}/_{2}$

CHARTS

Fair Isle and other color knitting is directed by a chart. Each square represents one stitch and one row. Colors are represented by symbols.

Odd-numbered rows are knit rows, even-numbered rows are purl rows. Read knit rows from right to left and purl rows from left to right (unless otherwise instructed).

YARNS

Rowan yarns, made in Britain, are specified for the garments in this book. The quality called "double knitting" (abbreviated DK) is a smooth yarn, thicker than sport weight and thinner than knitting worsted. A "four-ply" yarn is thinner than a sport weight. For best results, you should use the recommended yarn.

If you are unable to obtain the Rowan yarn specified, if may be possible to substitute another British or Continental yarn of the same type; ask the yarn salesperson for guidance.

Standard abbreviations

A to F	contrasting colors
alt	alternate(ly)
approx	approximate(ly)
beg	begin(ning)
cm	centimeter(s)
cont	continu(e) (ing)
dec	decreas(e) (ing)
foll	following
g	gram(s)
g st	garter stitch
in	inch(es)
inc	increas(e) (ing)
K	knit
MC	main color
mm	millimeters
P	purl
patt	pattern
psso	pass slipped stitch over
rem	remain(ing)
rep	repeat(ing)
sl	slip
st(s)	stitch(es)
st st	stockinette stitch
tbl	through back of loop(s)
tog	together

SIMPLE CLASSICS

THE DESIGNS IN this section are not only the essentials of any child's wardrobe but also simple enough for even the beginner to knit successfully. Whether smart or casual, for parties or for sportswear, each one has a distinctly stylish air. In many cases it is the addition of a special finishing touch that sets the pullover apart from the ordinary. These simple patterns are also ideal starting points for your imagination, as you can adapt and elaborate on them in whatever way you like.

Elizabeth's Pullover

MEASUREMENTS

To fit approx age 6 mths (2 yrs:4 yrs).
Actual chest measurement 48(58.5:63.5)cm [19(23:25)in].
Length 25.5(31.5:35.5)cm [10(12^1/$_2$:14)in].
Sleeve seam 19(23:28)cm [7^1/$_2$(9:11)in].

MATERIALS

Rowan Lightweight Double Knitting 25g hanks: 5(6:7) hanks.
1 pair each of 2^3/$_4$mm (size 2) and 3^1/$_4$mm (size 3) knitting needles.
A 2^3/$_4$mm (size 2) set of 4 double-pointed knitting needles.
3 small buttons.
Purchased collar (optional).

GAUGE

26 sts and 34 rows to 10cm (4in) square over st st on 3^1/$_4$mm (size 3) needles.

BACK

** With 2^3/$_4$mm (size 2) needles cast on 54(68:74) sts.
Work in K1, P1 rib for 4(5:5)cm [1^1/$_2$(2:2)in] inc to 62(76:82) sts in last row.
Change to 3^1/$_4$mm (size 3) needles.
Beg K row, work in st st until back measures 15(20.5:23)cm [6(8:9)in], ending P row.

Shape armholes. Bind off 2(3:3) sts at beg of next 2 rows. Dec one st each end of every row to 52(62:68) sts **.
Work straight until armholes measure 5(6.5:7.5)cm [2(2^1/$_2$:3)in], ending P row.

Back neck opening. NEXT ROW K22(27:30), then [P1, K1] 4 times for buttonhole band, turn and leave rem sts on a spare needle.
Work straight on first set of sts, working inner 8 sts in rib as set and rem sts in st st, until armhole measures 10(11.5:12.5)cm [4(4^1/$_2$:5)in], ending armhole edge, AT THE SAME TIME, make 2 buttonholes 2cm (^{3}/$_4$in) and 4cm (1^1/$_2$in) from beg of band as follows:
BUTTONHOLE ROW 1 (right side) Patt to last 5 sts, bind off 2, patt to end.
BUTTONHOLE ROW 2 Patt, casting on 2 sts over those bound off.

Shape shoulder. Bind off 6(8:9) sts at beg of next and foll alt row. Leave rem sts on a holder.
With right side facing join yarn to rem sts, bind on 8 sts and work [K1, P1] 4 times across these 8 sts for button band, then K sts on spare needle. Complete to match first side, omitting buttonholes.

FRONT

Work as given for back from ** to **.
Work straight until front measures 8(8:10) rows **less** than back to beg of shoulder shaping, ending P row.

Shape neck. NEXT ROW K20(25:28), turn and leave rem sts on a spare needle.
Bind off 3 sts at neck edge on next row, then 2 sts on foll alt row. Dec one st at neck edge on every row to 12(16:18) sts.
Work 1(0:1) row straight, ending armhole edge.

Shape shoulder. Bind off 6(8:9) sts at beg of next row. Work 1 row. Bind off.
With right side facing, sl center 12 sts on a holder, join yarn to rem sts, K to end. Work 1 row. Complete to match first side.

SLEEVES

With 2^3/$_4$mm (size 2) needles, cast on 32(34:40) sts.
Work in K1, P1 rib for 4(5:5)cm [1^1/$_2$(2:2)in].
Change to 3^1/$_4$mm (size 3) needles.
Beg K row and working in st st, inc one st each end of 3rd and every foll 5th(4th:5th) row to 46(58:66) sts.
Work straight until sleeve measures 19(23:28)cm [7^1/$_2$(9:11)in], ending P row.

Shape top. Bind off 2(3:3) sts at beg of next 2 rows.
Dec one st each end of every row to 36(46:54) sts, then every foll alt row to 30(38:46) sts, then on every row to 16(20:20) sts. Bind off 2(3:3) sts at beg of next 2 rows, then 3 sts at beg of foll 2 rows. Bind off.

NECKBAND

Join shoulder seams.
With the 2^3/$_4$mm (size 2) set of 4 double-pointed needles

and right side facing, rib across button band sts, then K left back neck sts inc 2 sts, pick up 13(14:16) sts down left front neck, K front neck sts inc 1 st, pick up 13(14:16) sts up right front neck, K right back neck sts inc 2 sts, then rib across buttonhole band sts. 79(83:89) sts. Turn.
Work backwards and forwards in rows of rib for 6 rows, making a buttonhole as before on 2nd and 3rd rows.
Using a 3^1/$_4$mm (size 3) needle, bind off loosely in rib.

TO MAKE UP
Set in sleeves. Join side and sleeve seams. Sew cast-on edge of button band behind buttonhole band at base. Sew on buttons. Sew on collar if desired.

Jack's Pullover

Shown on page 10

MEASUREMENTS
To fit approx age 6 mths (2 yrs:4 yrs).
Actual chest measurement 48(58.5:63.5)cm [19(23:25)in].
Length 30.5(37:40.5)cm [12(14^1/$_2$:16)in].
Sleeve seam 19(23:28)cm [7^1/$_2$(9:11)in].

MATERIALS
Rowan Lightweight Double Knitting 25g hanks; 5(6:7) hanks.
1 pair each of 2^3/$_4$mm (size 2) and 3^1/$_4$mm (size 3) knitting needles.

GAUGE
26 sts and 34 rows to 10cm (4in) square over st st on 3^1/$_4$mm (size 3) needles.

BACK
** With 2^3/$_4$mm (size 2) needles cast on 54(68:74) sts.
Work in K1, P1 rib for 4(5:5)cm [1^1/$_2$(2:2)in] inc to 62(76:82) sts in last row.
Change to 3^1/$_4$mm (size 3) needles.
Beg K row, work in st st until back measures 20.5(25.5:28)cm [8(10:11)in], ending P row **.

Shape armholes. Bind off 2(3:3) sts at beg of next 2 rows. Dec one st each end of every row to 52(62:68) sts.
Work straight until armholes measure 10(11.5:12.5)cm [4(4^1/$_2$:5)in], ending P row.

Shape shoulders. Bind off 6(8:9) sts at beg of next 4 rows. Leave rem sts on a holder.

FRONT
Work as given for back from ** to **.

Shape armhole and neck. NEXT ROW Bind off 2(3:3) sts, K next 28(34:37) sts, turn and leave rem sts on a

spare needle.
Dec one st at neck edge on next and every foll alt row, AT THE SAME TIME, dec one st at armhole edge on 2nd and foll 2(3:3) rows. 24(28:31) sts.
Keeping armhole edge straight, cont to dec at neck edge on every alt row from last dec to 15(21:25) sts, then on every foll 3rd row to 12(16:18) sts.
Work a few rows straight until front measures same as back to beg of shoulder shaping, ending armhole edge.

Shape shoulder. Bind off 6(8:9) sts at beg of next row. Work 1 row. Bind off.
With right side facing, join yarn to rem sts and K to end.
Bind off 2(3:3) sts at beg of next row. Complete to match first side.

SLEEVES
Work as given for sleeves of Elizabeth's pullover on page 12.

NECKBAND
Join right shoulder seam.
With 2^3/$_4$mm (size 2) needles and right side facing, pick up 33(37:41) sts down left front neck, one st at center front and mark this st, pick up 33(37:41) sts up right front neck, then K across back neck sts inc 4 sts. 99(109:119) sts.
RIB ROW (wrong side) K1, * P1, K1; rep from * to end.
Cont in rib as set for 1.5cm (^{1}/$_2$in), dec one st either side of center marked st on every row.
Bind off in rib, dec as before.

TO MAKE UP
Join left shoulder and neckband seam. Set in sleeves. Join side and sleeve seams.

Oliver's Cardigan

Shown on page 14

MEASUREMENTS
To fit approx age 6 mths (2 yrs:4 yrs).
Actual chest measurement 50(61:66)cm [19^3/$_4$(24:26)in].
Length 30.5(37:40.5)cm [12(14^1/$_2$:16)in].
Sleeve seam 19(23:28)cm [7^1/$_2$(9:11)in].

MATERIALS
Rowan Lightweight Double Knitting 25g hanks; 5(7:8) hanks.
1 pair each of 2^3/$_4$mm (size 2) and 3^1/$_4$mm (size 3) knitting needles.
4(5:5) buttons.

GAUGE
26 sts and 34 rows to 10cm (4in) square over st st on 3^1/$_4$mm (size 3) needles.

OLIVER'S CARDIGAN (INSTRUCTIONS BEGIN ON
PAGE 13)

BACK
Work as given for back of Jack's pullover.

LEFT FRONT
With 2³/₄mm (size 2) needles cast on 26(32:36) sts.
Work in K1, P1 rib for 4(5:5)cm [1¹/₂(2:2)in] inc to
30(37:40) sts in last row.
Change to 3¹/₄mm (size 3) needles.
Beg K row, work in st st until front measures same as
back to beg of armhole shaping, ending P row (for right
front end K row here).

Shape armhole and front neck. Bind off 2(3:3) sts
at beg of next row. Dec one st at neck edge on next and
every foll alt row, AT THE SAME TIME, dec one st at
armhole edge on 2nd and foll 2(3:3) rows.
23(27:30) sts.
Keeping armhole edge straight, cont to dec at neck
edge on every alt row from last dec to 16(22:26) sts,
then on every foll 3rd row to 12(16:18) sts.
Work a few rows straight until front measures same as
back to beg of shoulder shaping, ending armhole edge.

Shape shoulder. Bind off 6(8:9) sts at beg of next
row. Work 1 row. Bind off.

RIGHT FRONT
Work as for left front, noting exception in parentheses.

SLEEVES
Work as for sleeves of Elizabeth's pullover on page 12.

BUTTON BAND
Join shoulder seams.
With 2³/₄mm (size 2) needles cast on 11 sts.
Beg alt rows P1, work in K1, P1 rib until band, slightly
stretched, fits up front and across to center back neck.
Bind off in rib. Sew band in place.
Mark positions on band for 4(5:5) buttons, the first
approx 1.5cm (¹/₂in) from bind-on edge, the last at beg
of neck shaping and rem evenly spaced between.

BUTTONHOLE BAND
Work as given for button band making buttonholes to
match markers as follows:
BUTTONHOLE ROW 1 (right side) Rib 4, bind off 3, rib to
end.
BUTTONHOLE ROW 2 Rib, binding on 3 sts over those
bound off.

TO MAKE UP
Set in sleeves. Join side and sleeve seams. Join front
bands together at center back neck. Sew on buttons.

•

Chelsea's Cardigan

MEASUREMENTS
To fit approx age 6 mths (2 yrs:4 yrs).
Actual chest measurement 50 (61:66)cm
[19³/₄(24:26)in].
Length 25.5(31.5:35.5)cm [10(12¹/₂:14)in].
Sleeve seam 19(23:28)cm [7¹/₂(9:11)in].

MATERIALS
Rowan Lightweight Double Knitting 25g hanks; 5(7:8)
hanks.
1 pair each of 2³/₄mm (size 2) and 3¹/₄mm (size 3)
knitting needles.
5(6:7) buttons.
Approx 48(61:71)cm [19[24:28]in] of 2.5cm (1in)-wide
ribbon (optional).

GAUGE
26 sts and 34 rows to 10cm (4in) square over st st on
3¹/₄mm (size 3) needles.

BACK
With 2³/₄mm (size 2) needles cast on 54(68:74) sts.
Work in K1, P1 rib for 4(5:5)cm [1¹/₂(2:2)in] inc to
62(76:82) sts in last row.
Change to 3¹/₄mm (size 3) needles.
Beg K row, work in st st until back measures
15(20.5:23)cm [6(8:9)in], ending P row.

Shape armholes. Bind off 2(3:3) sts at beg of next 2
rows. Dec one st each end of every row to 52(62:68)
sts.
Work straight until armholes measure 10(11.5:12.5)cm
[4(4¹/₂:5)in], ending P row.

Shape shoulders. Bind off 6(8:9) sts at beg of next 4 rows. Leave rem sts on a holder.

LEFT FRONT

With 2¾mm (size 2) needles cast on 26(32:36) sts.
Work in K1, P1 rib for 4(5:5)cm [1½(2:2)in] inc to 30(37:40) sts in last row.
Change to 3¼mm (size 3) needles.
Beg K row, work in st st until front measures same as back to beg of armhole shaping, ending P row (for right front end with K row here).

Shape armhole. Bind off 2(3:3) sts at beg of next row. Work 1 row (omit this row when working right front).
Dec one st at armhole edge on every row to 25(30:33) sts.
Work straight until front measures 8(8:10) rows (for right front read 7(7:9) rows here) **less** than back to beg of shoulder shaping, ending armhole edge.

Shape neck. NEXT ROW Work 20(25:28) sts, turn and leave rem sts on a holder.
Bind off 3 sts at neck edge on next row, then 2 sts on foll alt row. Dec one st at neck edge on every row to 12(16:18) sts.
Work 1(0:1) row straight, ending armhole edge.

Shape shoulder. Bind off 6(8:9) sts at beg of next row. Work 1 row. Bind off.

RIGHT FRONT

Work as given for left front, noting exceptions in parentheses.

SLEEVES

Work as given for sleeves of Elizabeth's pullover on page 12.

BUTTON BAND

With 2¾mm (size 2) needles cast on 11 sts.
Beg alt rows P1, work in K1, P1 rib until band, slightly stretched, fits up front to beg of neck shaping. Leave sts on a holder. Sew band in place.
Mark positions on band for 4(5:6) buttons, the first approx 1.5cm (½in) from cast-on edge, the last approx 5(5.5:5)cm [2[2¼:2)in] from holder and rem evenly spaced between.

BUTTONHOLE BAND

Work as given for button band making buttonholes to match markers as follows:
BUTTONHOLE ROW 1 (right side) Rib 4, bind off 3, rib to end.
BUTTONHOLE ROW 2 Rib, casting on 3 sts over those bound off.

NECKBAND

Join shoulder seams.
With 2¾mm (size 2) needles and right side facing, rib across front band sts, then K right front neck sts inc one st, pick up 13(14:16) sts up right front neck, K back neck sts inc 3 sts, pick up 13(14:16) sts down left front neck, K left front neck sts inc one st, then rib across front band sts. 91(95:101) sts.
Work in rib as front bands for 6 rows making a buttonhole as before on rows 2 and 3. Using a 3¼mm (size 3) needle, bind off in rib.

TO MAKE UP

Set in sleeves. Join side and sleeve seams. Sew on buttons. If desired, sew a length of ribbon on front ribbed bands, turning in top and bottom edges. Cut buttonholes in ribbon to correspond with buttonholes. Either machine-stitch or blanket-stitch around button holes to finish.

CHELSEA IN HER
CARDIGAN TRIMMED WITH
TARTAN RIBBON

Fabian's Pullover

MEASUREMENTS
To fit approx age 6 mths (2 yrs:4 yrs).
Actual chest measurement 47(57:62)cm
[18$\frac{1}{2}$(22$\frac{1}{2}$:24$\frac{1}{2}$)in].
Length 25.5(31.5:35.5)cm [10(12$\frac{1}{2}$:14)in].

MATERIALS
Rowan Lightweight Double Knitting 25g hanks; 4(4:5)
hanks.
1 pair each of 2$\frac{3}{4}$mm (size 2) and 3$\frac{1}{4}$mm (size 3)
knitting needles; cable needle.

GAUGE
26 sts and 34 rows to 10cm (4in) square over st st on
3$\frac{1}{4}$mm (size 3) needles.
Cable measures approx 3cm (1$\frac{1}{4}$in).

SPECIAL ABBREVIATION
C8B = slip next 4 sts onto cable needle and leave at
back of work, K4, then K4 from cable needle.

Note If binding off over a cable, [work 2 tog] 4 times,
while binding off in usual way.

BACK
With 2$\frac{3}{4}$mm (size 2) needles cast on 54(68:74) sts.
Work in K1 tbl, P1 rib for 4(5:5)cm [1$\frac{1}{2}$(2:2)in] inc to
69(82:88) sts in last row.
Change to 3$\frac{1}{4}$mm (size 3) needles.
Work in patt as follows:
ROW 1 (right side) K8(11:12), P2, K8, P2, K29(36:40),
P2, K8, P2, K8(11:12).
ROW 2 P8(11:12), K2, P8, K2, P29(36:40), K2, P8m,
K2, P8(11:12).
ROWS 3 AND 4 As rows 1 and 2.
ROW 5 K8(11:12), P2, C8B, P2, K29(36:40), P2, C8B,
P2, K8(11:12).
ROW 6 As row 2.
ROWS 7 AND 8 As rows 1 and 2.
These 8 rows form the patt.
Cont in patt until front measures 15(20.5:23)cm
[6(8:9)in], ending wrong side row.

Shape armholes. Keeping patt correct, bind off
2(3:3) sts at beg of next 2 rows Dec one st each end of
every row to 55(66:72) sts.
Work straight until armholes measures
10(11.5:12.5)cm [4(4$\frac{1}{2}$:5)in], ending wrong side row.

Shape shoulders. Bind off 7(9:10) sts at beg of next 4
rows.
Leave rem sts on a holder.

•

CABLE BANDS DOWN EACH SIDE GIVE THIS
PULLOVER A TRIM-FITTING LOOK

FRONT
Work as back until front measures 12(12:14) rows **less**
than back to beg off shoulder shaping, ending wrong
side row.

Shape neck. NEXT ROW Patt 22(27:30), turn and leave
rem sts on a spare needle.
Bind off 3 sts at neck edge on next row, then 2 sts on
foll alt row. Dec one st at neck edge on every row to
14(18:20) sts.
Work 5(4:5) rows straight, ending armhole edge.

Shape shoulder. Bind off 7(9:10) sts at beg of next
row. Work 1 row. Bind off.
With right side facing slip center 11(12:12) sts on a
holder, join yarn to rem sts and K to end. Work 1 row.
Complete to match first side.

NECKBAND
Join right shoulder seam.
With 2$\frac{3}{4}$mm (size 2) needles and right side facing, pick
up 19(19:21) sts down left front neck, K front neck sts
inc 4 sts, pick up 19(19:21) sts up right front neck, K
back neck sts inc 6 sts. 86(90:96) sts.
Work in K1 tbl, P1 rib for 1.5cm ($\frac{1}{2}$in). With 3$\frac{1}{4}$mm
(size 3) needle, bind off loosely in rib.

ARMHOLE BANDS
Join left shoulder and neckband seams.
With 2$\frac{3}{4}$mm (size 2) needles and right side facing, pick
78(84:92) sts around armhole edge.
Work in K1 tbl, P1 rib 1.5cm ($\frac{1}{2}$in), dec one st each end
of every row. Bind off in rib.

TO MAKE UP
Join side and armhole band seams.

Julian's Pullover

Shown on page 19, second from left.

MEASUREMENTS
To fit approx age 6 mths (2 yrs:4 yrs).
Actual chest measurement (unstretched)
47(57:61.5)cm[18$\frac{1}{2}$(22$\frac{1}{2}$:24$\frac{1}{2}$)in].
Length 30.5(37:40.5)cm [12(14$\frac{1}{2}$:16)in].
Sleeve seam approx 19(23:28)cm [7$\frac{1}{2}$(9:11)in].

MATERIALS
Rowan Lightweight Double Knitting 25g hanks;
Main color (MC) Cream (02) 8(9:10) hanks, 1st
contrasting color (A) Navy (97) 1(1:1) hank, 2nd
contrasting color (B) Blue (51) 1(1:1) hank.
1 pair each of 2$\frac{3}{4}$mm (size 2) and 3$\frac{1}{4}$mm (size 3)
knitting needles.
Cable needle.

GAUGE
36 sts and 40 rows to 10cm (4in) square over patt
(unstretched) on 3$\frac{1}{4}$mm (size 3) needles.

1 7

SPECIAL ABBREVIATION
C6F = sl next 3 sts onto cable needle and leave at front of work, K3, then K3 from cable needle.

Note If binding off over a cable, [work 2 tog] 3 times, while binding off in usual way.

BACK
With 2³/₄mm (size 2) needles and MC, cast on 54(68:74) sts.
Work in K1, P1 rib for 4(6:6) rows.
Change to A, K 1 row, then rib 2 rows, change to MC, P 1 row, then rib 2 rows, change to B, K 1 row, then rib 2 rows, change to MC, P 1 row, then cont in MC only until rib measures 4(5:5)cm [1¹/₂(2:2)in] inc to 84(104:110) sts in last row.
Change to 3¹/₄mm (size 3) needles.
ROW 1 (right side) P3(2:5), K1, P2, * K6, P2, K1, P2; rep from * to last 1(0:3) sts, P1(0:3).
ROW 2 K6(5:8), * P6, K5; rep from * to last 1(0:3) sts, K1(0:3).
ROW 3 P3(2:5), K1, P2, * C6F, P2, K1, P2; rep from * to last 1(0:3) sts, P1(0:3).
ROW 4 As row 2.
ROWS 5 AND 6 As rows 1 and 2.
These 6 rows form the patt.
Cont in patt until back measures 20.5(25.5:28)cm [8(10:11)in], ending wrong side row.

Shape armholes. Keeping patt correct, bind off 3(5:5) sts at beg of next 2 rows. Dec one st each end of next 3(5:5) rows. 72(84:90) sts.
Work straight until armholes measure 10(11.5:12.5)cm [4(4¹/₂:5)in], ending wrong side row.

Shape shoulders. Bind off 9(11:12) sts at beg of next 2 rows, then 8(11:12) sts at beg of foll 2 rows. Leave rem sts on a holder.

FRONT
Work as back until front measures 4 rows **less** than back to beg of armhole shaping, ending wrong side row.

Shape neck. **NEXT ROW** Patt 42(52:55), turn and leave rem sts on a spare needle.
Keeping patt correct, dec one st at neck edge on next and foll alt row. 40(50:53) sts.

Shape armhole. Bind off 3(5:5) sts at beg of next row. Cont to dec at neck edge on every alt row from last dec, AT THE SAME TIME, dec one st at armhole edge on 2nd and 2(4:4) foll rows. 32(37:40) sts.
Keeping armhole edge straight, cont to dec at neck edge on every foll alt row from last dec to 17(26:31) sts, then on **2nd and 3rd sizes only** dec one st at neck edge on every foll 3rd row to (22:24) sts.
On all sizes, work a few rows straight until front measures same as back to beg of shoulder shaping, ending armhole edge.

Shape shoulder. Bind off 9(11:12) sts at beg of next row. Work 1 row. Bind off.
With right side facing, join yarn to rem sts and patt to end. Dec one st at neck edge on next and foll alt row. Work 1 row.

Shape armhole. Bind off 3(5:5) sts, patt to last 2 sts work 2 tog.
Cont to dec at neck edge on every alt row from last dec, AT THE SAME TIME, dec one st at armhole edge on next 3(5:5) rows. 32(37:40) sts.
Complete to match first side.

SLEEVES
With 2³/₄mm (size 2) needles and MC, cast on 30(34:40) sts.
Work in K1, P1 rib in MC only until rib measures 4(5:5)cm [1¹/₂(2:2)in] inc to 42(46:53) sts in last row.
Change to 3¹/₄mm (size 3) needles.
ROW 1 (right side) K2(4:2), P2, K1, P2, * K6, P2, K1, P2; rep from * to last 2(4:2) sts, K2(4:2).
ROW 2 P2(4:2), K5, * P6, K5; rep from * to last 2(4:2) sts, P2(4:2).
Cont in patt as set, inc one st each end of next and every foll 5th(3rd:4th) row to 62(60:73) sts, then on **2nd and 3rd sizes only** inc one st on every foll (4th:5th) row to (80:90) sts, working inc sts in patt on **all sizes**.
Work straight until sleeve measures approx 19(23:28)cm [7¹/₂(9:11)in], ending wrong side row and same cable patt row as back to beg of armhole shaping.

Shape top. Keeping patt correct, bind off 3(5:5) sts at beg of next 2 rows.
Dec one st each end of every row to 50(64:74) sts, then each end of every foll alt row to 46(60:70) sts, then each end of every row to 24(24:26) sts. Bind off 4(5:5) sts at beg of next 2 rows, then 4 sts at beg of foll 2 rows. Bind off.

NECKBAND
Join right shoulder seam.
With 2³/₄mm (size 2) needles and right side facing and MC, pick up 35(39:43) sts down left front neck, pick up one st from center front and mark this st, pick up 36(40:44) sts up right front neck, then K back neck sts dec 3 sts across each group of cables. 101(111:121) sts.
RIB ROW (wrong side) K1, * P1, K1; rep from * to end.
This row sets the rib.
Change to B, K 1 row, then rib 2 rows, change to A, P 1 row, then rib 2 rows, change to MC, K 1 row, then rib 2 rows, AT THE SAME TIME, dec one st either side of center marked st on every row.
With MC, bind off in rib, dec as before.

TO MAKE UP
Join left shoulder and neckband seam. Set in sleeves. Join side and sleeve seams.

LEFT TO RIGHT: HAL, JULIAN, OLIVER, AND FABIAN IN THEIR SMART CRICKETING KNITS

•

Oliver's Pullover

To fit approx age 6 mths (2 yrs:4 yrs).
Actual chest measurement (unstretched)
47(57:61.5)cm[$18^1/_2$($22^1/_2$:$24^1/_2$)in].
Length 30.5(37:40.5)cm [12($14^1/_2$:16)in].

MATERIALS
Rowan Lightweight Double Knitting 25g hanks; Main
color (MC) Cream (02) 6(7:8) hanks, 1st contrasting
color (A) Mid-blue (52) 1(1:1) hank, 2nd contrasting
color (B) Light blue (49) 1(1:1) hank.
1 pair each of $2^3/_4$mm (size 2) and $3^1/_4$mm (size 3)
knitting needles.
Cable needle.

GAUGE
36 sts and 40 rows to 10cm (4in) square over patt
(unstretched) on $3^1/_4$mm (size 3) needles.

SPECIAL ABBREVIATION
C6F = sl next 3 sts onto cable needle and leave at front
of work, K3, then K3 from cable needle.

Note If binding off over a cable, [work 2 tog] 3 times,
while binding off in usual way.

BACK, FRONT, AND NECKBAND
Work as given for back, front, and neckband of Julian's
pullover (page 17).

ARMHOLE BANDS
Join left shoulder and neckband seam.
With $2^3/_4$mm (size 2) needles and MC, pick up 76(86:92)
sts around armhole edge.
Work in K1, P1 rib in MC for 1.5cm ($^1/_2$in), dec one st
each end of every row. Bind off in rib.

TO MAKE UP
Join side and armhole band seams.

Louisa's Pullover

MEASUREMENTS
To fit approx age 6 mths (2 yrs:4 yrs).
Actual chest measurement 48(58.5:63.5)cm
[19(23:25)in].
Length 25.5(31.5:35.5)cm [10(12½:14)in].
Sleeve seam 19(23:28)cm [7½(9:11)in].

MATERIALS
Rowan's Edina Ronay Silk and Wool 20g balls; Main
color (MC) Oatmeal (854) 5(7:8) balls, contrasting color
(A) Navy (848) or Red (842) 1(1:1) ball.
1 pair each of 2¼mm (size 1) and 3mm (size 2) knitting
needles.
4(6:6) small buttons.

GAUGE
32 sts and 42 rows to 10cm (4in) square over st st on
3mm (size 2) needles.

BACK
With 2¼mm (size 1) needles and MC, cast on 70(84:92)
sts.
Work in K1 tb1, P1 rib for 4(5:5)cm [1½(2:2)in] inc to
76(92:100) sts in last row.
Change to 3mm (size 2) needles.
Beg K row, work in st st until back measures
15(20.5:23)cm [6(8:9)in], ending P row.

Shape armholes. Bind off 4 sts at beg of next 2 rows.
Dec one st each end of every row to 62(78:86) sts, then
every foll alt row to 60(72:80) sts.
Work straight until armholes measure 10(11.5:12.5)cm
[4(4½:5)in], ending P row.

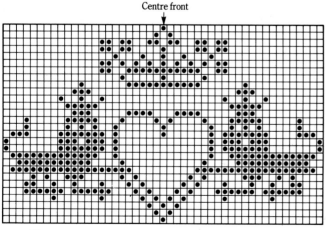

Key
□ = MC
◉ = Swiss embroider in A

THE CHART ABOVE IS WORKED ON THE PULLOVER
FRONTS IN DUPLICATE STITCH

Shape shoulders. Bind off 13(18:21) sts at beg of
next 2 rows.

Back neckband. Change to 2¼mm (size 1) needles
and A. K 7 rows on rem 34(36:38) sts. Bind off.

FRONT
Work as given for back until front measures 10 rows
less than back to beg of shoulder shaping, ending P
row.

Shape neck. NEXT ROW K24(29:32), turn and leave
rem sts on a spare needle.

ARABELLA WEARS A BONNET (SEE PAGE 23) TO MATCH HER SMALLER VERSION OF THE SWEATER

•

Bind off 3 sts at neck edge on next row, then 2 sts on foll alt row. Dec one st at neck edge on every row to 13(18:21) sts, ending armhole edge.

Buttonhole band. K 2 rows.
BUTTONHOLE ROW 1 K5(5:6), bind off 2, K next 0(4:5) sts, bind off 0(2:2), K to end.
BUTTONHOLE ROW 2 K casting on 2 sts over those bound off. K 3 rows. Bind off.
With right side facing sl center 12(14:16) sts on a holder, join yarn to rem sts and K to end. Work 1 row. Complete to match first side.

SLEEVES

With 2¼mm (size 1) needles and MC, cast on 38(42:48) sts.
Work in K1 tbl, P1 rib for 4(5:5)cm [1½(2:2)in].
Change to 3mm (size 2) needles.
Beg K row, work in st st, inc one st each end of 5th and every foll 5th(4th:5th) row to 56(72:80) sts.
Work straight until sleeve measures 19(23:28)cm [7½(9:11)in], ending P row.

Shape sleeve top. Bind off 4 sts at beg of next 2 rows. Dec one st each end of every row to 40(54:62)

THE SWEATER WITH DUPLICATE STITCH LOOKS JUST AS SMART ON A BOY

•

sts, then on every foll alt row to 26(42:50) sts, then on every row to 22(24:24) sts. Bind off 3 sts at beg of next 4 rows. Bind off.

FRONT NECKBAND
With 2¼mm (size 1) needles, right side facing and A, pick up 15 sts down left front neck including row ends of buttonhole band, K front neck sts, pick up 15 sts up right front neck including row ends of buttonhole band. 42(44:46) sts. K 2 rows.
BUTTONHOLE ROW 1 K3, bind off 2, K to last 5 sts, bind off 2, K3.

BUTTONHOLE ROW 2 K casting on 2 sts over those bound off.
K 4 rows. Bind off.

TO MAKE UP
Duplicate stitch crest motif in A from chart on center front of sweater, ending top of motif approx 4cm (1½in) from top of neckband. Embroider chosen letters in heart as shown in the picture. Lapping buttonhole bands over back shoulders, join row ends together at armhole edge. Set in sleeves. Join side and sleeve seams. Sew on buttons.

Arabella's Bonnet

MEASUREMENTS
To fit approx age 6 mths to 1 yr.
Depth approx 15cm (6in) from crown to center front.

MATERIALS
Rowan's Edina Ronay Silk and Wool 20g balls; Main color (MC) Ecru (857) 1 ball, contrasting color (A) Red (842) 1 ball.
1 pair each of 2^{1}/$_{4}$mm (size 1) and 3mm (size 2) knitting needles.
A 3mm (size 2) set of 4 double-pointed needles.
Approx 66cm (26in) of 2cm/^{3}/$_{4}$in-wide double-faced satin ribbon.

GAUGE
32 sts and 42 rows to 10cm (4in) square over st st on 3mm (size 2) needles.

With 3mm (size 2) needles and MC, cast on 85 sts and K 4 rows.
NEXT ROW K.
NEXT ROW K3, P to last 3 sts, K3.
Rep the last 2 rows until work measures 7.5cm (3in), casting on 25 sts at beg of last row for center back neck. 110 sts.
Change to 3 mm (size 2) set of 4 needles, and placing a marker at beg of round, work in ROUNDS as follows:
NEXT ROUND K to last 25 sts, P these sts for center back neck.
NEXT ROUND K.
NEXT ROUND K to last 25 sts, P these sts for center back neck.
Now work in st st (K every round) until work measures 10cm (4in).

Shape crown. NEXT ROUND * K9, K2 tog; rep from * to end.
NEXT AND EVERY FOLL ALT ROUND K.
NEXT ROUND * K8, K2 tog; rep from * to end.
NEXT ALT ROUND * K7, K2 tog; rep from * to end.
NEXT ALT ROUND * K6, K2 tog; rep from * to end.
Cont to dec as set on every alt round, working one st **less** in each rep to 20 sts.
NEXT ROUND K.
NEXT ROUND [K2 tog] to end. 10 sts.
Break off yarn, leaving an end. Thread end through rem sts, draw up tightly and secure.
With 2^{1}/$_{4}$mm (size 1) needles, right side facing and MC, pick up 25 sts from the 25 cast-on sts at center back neck.
Beg alt rows P1, work in K1, P1 rib for 2.5cm (1in). Leave sts on a holder.

EDGING
Join row ends of back rib to row ends of main part of bonnet.
With 3mm (size 2) set of 4 needles and A, pick up 130 sts all around outer edge of bonnet including back neck sts on holder.
Work in **rounds** as follows:
K 1 round, then P 4 rounds. Bind off knitwise.

TO MAKE UP
Duplicate stitch motif in A from chart on center front of bonnet.
Sew ribbon in two, fold under ends, to sides of bonnet, gathering ends to form rosettes.

Centre front

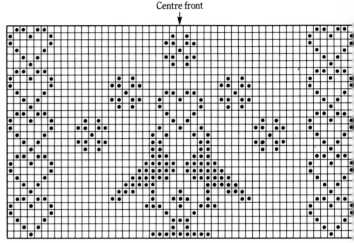

Key
□ = MC
▣ = Swiss embroider in A

WORK THIS BIRDS AND HEART MOTIF IN DUPLICATE STITCH

Hal and Oliver's cardigans
Shown on page 24

MEASUREMENTS
To fit approx age 6 mths (2 yrs:4 yrs).
Actual chest measurement 48(58.5:63.5)cm [19(23:25)in].
Length 25.5(31.5:35.5)cm [10(12^{1}/$_{2}$:14)in].
Sleeve seam 19(23:28)cm [7^{1}/$_{2}$(9:11)in].

MATERIALS
Rowan Lightweight Double Knitting 25g hanks; 10(11:12) hanks.
1 pair each of 2^{3}/$_{4}$mm (size 2) and 3^{1}/$_{4}$mm (size 3) knitting needles.
4 buttons.

GAUGE
26 sts and 34 rows to 10cm (4in) square over st st on 3^{1}/$_{4}$mm (size 3) needles.

BACK
Work as given for back of Chelsea's cardigan (page 14), but bind off rem center back neck sts.

LEFT FRONT

With 2³/₄mm (size 2) needles cast on 42(50:54) sts.
Work in K1, P1 rib for 4(5:5)cm [1¹/₂(2:2)in] inc 3 sts
over last 14(20:22) sts (for right front read first
14(20:22) sts here) on last row. 45(53:57) sts.
Change to 3¹/₄mm (size 3) needles.
ROW 1 (right side) K.
ROW 2 K28 (30:32), P17(23:25).
Rep last 2 rows until front measures same as back to
armholes, ending wrong side row (for right front end
right side row here).

Shape armhole. Keeping front garter st border
correct, bind off 2(3:3) sts at beg of next row.
Work 1 row (for right front omit this row).
Dec one st at armhole edge on every row to 40(46:50)
sts.
Work straight until armhole measures same as back to
beg of shoulder shaping, ending armhole edge.

Shape shoulder. Bind off 6(8:9) sts at beg of next row
and foll alt row. 28(30:32) sts.
Cont straight on rem sts until garter st border fits
across to center back neck, ending right side row (for
right front end wrong side row here).

Shape border. NEXT 2 ROWS K24(26:28), turn, sl 1, K
to end.
NEXT 2 ROWS K20(22:24), turn, sl 1, K to end.
NEXT 2 ROWS K16(18:20), turn, sl 1, K to end.
Cont in this way until the rows K4(2:4), turn, sl 1, K to
end have been worked.
Bind off.

RIGHT FRONT

Work as given for left front, noting exceptions in
parentheses, reversing garter st front border and
making buttonholes when front measures approx 2.5cm
(1in) and 7.5(9:10)cm [3(3¹/₂:4)in] from beg as follows:
BUTTONHOLE ROW 1 (right side) Patt 7, bind off 3, patt
next 7(9:11) sts, bind off 3, patt to end.
BUTTONHOLE ROW 2 Patt, casting on 3 sts over those
bound off.

SLEEVES

Work as given for sleeves of Elizabeth's pullover (page
12).

TO MAKE UP

Join shoulder seams. Join bound-off edges of garter st
border together, then sew row ends of border to back
neck. Set in sleeves. Join side and sleeve seams. Sew
on buttons.

•

HAL AND OLIVER IN THEIR BRASS-BUTTONED
DOUBLE-BREASTED CARDIGANS

MATCHING BERET
Shown on page 11

MEASUREMENT
To suit approx age 6 mths (2 to 4 yrs)

MATERIALS
Rowan Lightweight Double Knitting 25g hanks; 1(2)
hanks.
1 pair each of 3mm (size 2) knitting needles.

GAUGE
28 sts and 35 rows to 10cm (4in) square over st st on
3mm (size 2) needles.

SPECIAL ABBREVIATION
kw = knitwise.

With 3mm (size 2) needles cast on 94(139) sts.
NEXT ROW (right side) K3, inc kw in next st, K9(14);
rep from * to last st, K1.
NEXT AND EVERY FOLL ALT ROW P.
NEXT ROW K3, inc kw in next st, K10(15); rep from * to
last st, K1.
NEXT ROW K3, inc kw in next st, K11(16); rep from * to
last st, K1.
NEXT ROW K3, inc kw in next st, K12(17); rep from * to
last st, K1.
NEXT ROW K3, inc kw in next st, K13(18); rep from * to
last st, K1.
NEXT ROW K3, inc kw in next st, K14(19); rep from * to
last st, K1.
2ND SIZE ONLY
NEXT ROW K3, inc kw in next st, K20; rep from * to last
st, K1.
BOTH SIZES NEXT ROW P. 148(202) sts.

Shape crown. NEXT ROW K3, * sl 1, K1, psso,
K14(20); rep from * to last st, K1.
NEXT AND EVERY FOLL ALT ROW P.
NEXT ROW K3, * sl 1, K1, psso, K13(19); rep from * to
last st, K1.
NEXT ROW K3, * sl 1, K1, psso, K12(18); rep from * to
last st, K1.
Cont to dec as set working one st less in each rep to 22
sts.
NEXT ROW P.
NEXT ROW [Sl 1, K1, psso] to end. 11 sts.
Break off yarn leaving an end. Run end through rem
sts, draw up tightly and secure.

RIBBING
With 3mm (size 2) needles and right side facing, pick up
70(110) sts from cast-on edge.
Work in K1, P1 rib for 10 rows. Bind off loosely in rib.

TO MAKE UP
Join back seam. If necessary, run a few rows of shirring
elastic through ribbing to give a firmer fit.

CABLES

WHEN IT COMES to warm outdoor sweaters, you cannot do better than classic cable and Aran designs. They look equally smart on boys or girls and can be worn either for casual or special occasions. You can knit them short or long, and the range of patterns here ranges from a lightweight vest to a smart collared jacket. Knitted up in different styles and colors, the same basic cabling techniques will produce a whole host of different sweaters.

Hal's Pullover

Shown on page 26, left

MEASUREMENTS

To fit approx age 6 mths (2 yrs:4 yrs).
Actual chest measurement 48(58.5:63.5)cm
[19(23:25)in].
Length 30.5(37:40.5)cm [12(14^1/$_2$:16)in].
Sleeve seam 19(23:28)cm [7^1/$_2$(9:11)in].

MATERIALS

Rowan Lightweight Double Knitting 25g hanks;
10(10:11) hanks.
1 pair each of 2^3/$_4$mm (size 2) and 3^1/$_4$mm (size 3)
knitting needles.
Cable needle.

GAUGE

34 sts and 40 rows to 10cm (4in) square over patt
(slightly stretched) on 3^1/$_4$mm (size 3) needles.

SPECIAL ABBREVIATIONS

C4B = sl next 2 sts onto cable needle and leave at back
of work, K2, then K2 from cable needle.
C6B = sl next 3 sts onto cable needle and leave at back
of work, K3, then K3 from cable needle.
Note If binding off over a cable, [work 2 tog] 3 times,
while binding off in usual way.

BACK

With 2^3/$_4$mm (size 2) needles cast on 55(64:75) sts.
P 1 row and K 1 row.
Now work in fancy rib as follows:
RIB ROW 1 (right side) K2(2:3), P1, * K4, P1, K3, P1;
rep from * to last 7(7:8) sts, K4, P1, K2(2:3).
RIB ROW 2 P2(2:3), K1, * P4, K1, P3, K1; rep from * to
last 7[7:8] sts, P4, K1, P2(2:3).
RIB ROW 3 P3(3:4), * K4, P5; rep from * to last 7(7:8)
sts, K4, P3(3:4).
RIB ROW 4 As row 2.
RIB ROW 5 K2(2:3), P1, * C4B, P1, K3, P1; rep from *
to last 7(7:8) sts, C4B, P1, K2(2:3).
RIB ROW 6 K3(3:4), * P4, K5; rep from * to last 7(7:8)
sts, P4, K3(3:4).
Cont in fancy rib until waistband measures 4(5:5)cm
[1^1/$_2$(2:2)in], ending wrong side row and inc to
80(98:106) sts in last row.
Change to 3^1/$_4$mm (size 3) needles.
Work in patt as follows:
ROW 1 (right side) K0(2:0), P0(3:0), K0(1:0), P0(3:0),
K1(1:0), P3(3:0), K3(3:0), P3(3:0), K1, P3, * K6, P3,
K1, P3, K3, P3, K1, P3; rep from * to last 20(6:10)
sts, K6(1:6), P3, K1(2:1), P3(0:0), K3(0:0), P3(0:0),
K1(0:0).
ROW 2 P0(2:0), K0(3:0), P0(1:0), K0(3:0), P1(1:0),
K3(3:0), P3(3:0), K3(3:0), P1, K3, * P6, K3, P1, K3,
P3, K3, P1, K3; rep from * to last 20(6:10) sts,
P6(1:6), K3, P1(2:1), K3(0:0), P3(0:0), K3(0:0),
P1(0:0).

ROW 3 As row 1.
ROW 4 K14(23:4), * P6, K17; rep from * to last
20(6:10) sts, P6(0:6), K14(6:4).
ROW 5 K0(2:0), P0(3:0), K0(1:0), P0(3:0), K1(1:0),
P3(3:0), K3(3:0), P3(3:0), K1, P3, * C6B, P3, K1, P3,
K3, P3, K1, P3; rep from * to last 20(6:10) sts,
C6B(0:C6B), K0(1:0), P3, K1(2:1), P3(0:0), K3(0:0),
P3(0:0), K1(0:0).
ROW 6 As row 2.
ROWS 7 AND 8 As rows 1 and 4.
These 8 rows form the patt.
Cont in patt until back measures 20.5(25.5:28)cm
[8(10:11)in], ending wrong side row.

Shape armholes. Keeping patt correct, bind off
6(9:10) sts at beg of next 2 rows. 68(80:86) sts.
Work straight until armholes measure 10(11.5:12.5)cm
[4(4^1/$_2$:5)in], ending wrong side row.
NEXT ROW Bind off 16(21:23) sts, patt to last 16(21:23)
sts and bind off these sts. Leave rem sts on a holder.

FRONT

Work as given for back until armholes measure
5.5(6.5:7)cm [2^1/$_4$(2^1/$_2$:2^3/$_4$)in], ending wrong side row.

Shape neck. NEXT ROW Patt 26(31:33), turn and leave
rem sts on a spare needle.
Keeping patt correct, bind off 2 sts at neck edge on
next and foll alt row. Dec one st at neck edge on every
foll alt row to 16(21:23) sts.
Work a few rows straight until armhole measures same
as back to shoulder, ending wrong side row.
Bind off.
With right side facing, sl center 16(18:20) sts on a
holder, join yarn to rem sts and patt to end.
Work 1 row. Complete to match first side.

SLEEVES

With 2^3/$_4$mm (size 2) needles cast on 28(28:30) sts.
P 1 row and K 1 row.
Now work in fancy rib as given for back for 4(5:5)cm
[1^1/$_2$(2:2)in], ending wrong side row and inc to 43(43:51)
sts in last row.
Change to 3^1/$_4$mm (size 3) needles.
Work in patt as follows.
ROW 1 (right side) P0(0:1), K0(0:3), P3, K1, P3, K6,
P3, K1, P3, K3, P3, K1, P3, K6, P3, K1, P3, K0(0:3),
P0(0:1).
ROW 2 K0(0:1), P0(0:3), K3, P1, K3, P6, K3, P1, K3,
P3, K3, P1, K3, P6, K3, P1, K3, P0(0:3), K0(0:1).
ROW 3 As row 1.
ROW 4 K7(7:11), P6, K17, P6, K7(7:11).
Cont in patt as set, working as back, inc one st each end
of next, then every foll 3rd(3rd:4th) row to 49(61:63)
sts, then on every foll 5th(4th:5th) row to 69(77:85)
sts, working inc sts in patt.
Work straight until sleeve measures 19(23:28)cm
[7^1/$_2$(9:11)in], ending wrong side row. Place a marker
each end of last row. Work another 8(10:12) rows. Bind
off.

NECKBAND

Join right shoulder seam.
With 2³/₄mm (size 2) needles and right side facing, pick up 15(16:16) sts down left front neck, K front neck sts but on **3rd size only** dec one st each end, pick up 15(16:16) sts up right front neck, then K back neck sts dec 4(5:1) sts. 78(83:89) sts.
Work in fancy rib as follows:
RIB ROW 1 (wrong side) P0(1:0), K0(1:0), P3(4:3), * K1, P3, K1, P4, rep from * to last 3(5:5) sts, K1, P2(3:3), K0(1:1).
Cont in fancy rib as set for 5.5(6.5:7.5)cm [2¹/₄(2¹/₂:3)in].
With 3¹/₄mm (size 3) needles, bind off loosely in rib.

TO MAKE UP

Join left shoulder and neckband seam. Turn neckband in half to wrong side and sew in place. Set in sleeves, sewing row ends above markers to bound-off sts at underarms. Join side and sleeve seams.

Oliver's Pullover

Shown on page 26, right; and in white on Laura

MEASUREMENTS

To fit approx age 6 mths (2 yrs:4 yrs).
Actual chest measurement 48(58.5:63.5)cm [19(23:25)in].
Length 25.5(31.5:35.5)cm [10(12¹/₂:14)in].
Sleeve seam 19(23:28)cm [7¹/₂(9:11)in].

MATERIALS

Rowan Lightweight Double Knitting 25g hanks; 8(9:10) hanks.
1 pair each of 2³/₄mm (size 2) and 3¹/₄mm (size 3) knitting needles.
Cable needle.

GAUGE

34 sts and 40 rows to 10cm (4in) square over patt (slightly stretched) on 3¹/₄mm (size 3) needles.

SPECIAL ABBREVIATIONS

C4B = sl next 2 sts onto cable needle and leave at back of work, K2, then K2 from cable needle.
C6B = sl next 3 sts onto cable needle and leave at back of work, K3, then K3 from cable needle.

Note If binding off over a cable, [work 2 tog] 3 times, while binding off in usual way.

BACK, FRONT, SLEEVES, NECKBAND AND TO MAKE UP

Work as given for back, front, sleeves, neckband, and to make up of Hal's pullover (page 28), but working to 15(20.5:23)cm [6(8:9)in] before armhole shaping on back and front, ending wrong side row.

Ashley's Sweater

See page 30, right

MEASUREMENTS

To fit approx age 6 mths (2 yrs:4 yrs).
Actual chest measurement 48(58.5:63.5)cm [19(23:25)in].
Length 25.5(31.5:35.5)cm [10(12¹/₂:14)in].
Sleeve seam 19(23:28)cm [7¹/₂(9:11)in].

MATERIALS

Rowan Lightweight Double Knitting 25g hanks; 8(9:10) hanks.
1 pair each of 2³/₄mm (size 2) and 3¹/₄mm (size 3) knitting needles.
A 2³/₄mm (size 2) set of 4 double-pointed knitting needles.
Cable needle.

GAUGE

34 sts and 40 rows to 10cm (4in) square over patt (slightly stretched) on 3¹/₄mm (size 3) needles.

SPECIAL ABBREVIATION

C6B = slip next 3 sts onto cable needle and leave at back of work, K3, then K3 from cable needle.
Note If binding off over a cable, [work 2 tog] 3 times, while binding off in the usual way.

BACK

** With 2³/₄mm (size 2) needles cast on 54(66:78) sts.
RIB ROW 1 (right side) K2, * P2, K2; rep from * to end.
RIB ROW 2 P2, * K2, P2; rep from * to end.
Cont in rib until waistband measures 4(5:5)cm [1¹/₂(2:2)in], ending wrong side row and inc to 80(98:106) sts in last row. Change to 3¹/₄mm (size 3) needles.
Work in patt as follows:
ROW 1 (right side) K0(2:0), P0(3:0), K0(1:0), P0(3:0), K1(1:0), P3(3:0), K3(3:0), P3(3:0), K1, P3, * K6, P3, K1, P3, K3, P3, K1, P3; rep from * to last 20(6:10) sts, K6(1:6), P3, K1(2:1), P3(0:0), K3(0:0), P3(0:0), K1(0:0).
ROW 2 P0(2:0), K0(3:0), P0(1:0), K0(3:0), P1(1:0), K3(3:0), P3(3:0), K3(3:0), P1, K3, * P6, K3, P1, K3, P3, K3, P1, K3;rep from * to last 20(6:10) sts, P6(1:6), K3, P1(2:1), K3(0:0), P3(0:0), K3(0:0), P1(0:0).
ROW 3 As row 1.
ROW 4 K14(23:4), * P6, K17; rep from * to last 20(6:10) sts, P6(0:6), K14(6:4).
ROW 5 K0(2:0), P0(3:0), K0(1:0), P0(3:0), K1(1:0), P3(3:0), K3(3:0), P3(3:0), K1, P3, * C6B, P3, K1, P3, K3, P3, K1, P3; rep from * to last 20(6:10) sts, C6B(0:C6B), K0(1:0), P3, K1(2:1), P3(0:0), K3(0:0), P3(0:0), K1(0:0).
ROW 6 As row 2. **ROWS 7 AND 8** As rows 1 and 4.
These 8 rows form the patt.
Cont in patt until back measures 15(20.5:23)cm [6(8:9)in], ending wrong side row.

Shape armholes. Keeping patt correct, bind off 6(9:10) sts at beg of next 2 rows. 68(80:86) sts. **
Work straight until armholes measure 10(11.5:12.5)cm [4(4½:5)in], ending wrong side row.
NEXT ROW Bind off 16(21:23) sts, patt to last 16(21:23) sts and bind off these sts. Leave rem sts on a holder.

FRONT
Work as given for back from ** to **.

Shape neck. NEXT ROW Patt 16(21:23), turn and leave rem sts on a spare needle.
Work straight on these sts until armhole measures same as back to shoulder, ending wrong side row. Bind off. With right side facing, join yarn to rem sts, bind off center 36(38:40) sts and patt to end. Complete to match first side.

SLEEVES
With 2¾mm (size 2) needles cast on 32(32:36) sts.
Work in K2, P2, rib for 4(5:5)cm [1½(2:2)in], inc to 43(43:51) sts in last row.
Change to 3¼mm (size 3) needles.
Work in patt as follows.
ROW 1 (right side) P0(0:1), K0(0:3), P3, K1, P3, K6, P3, K1, P3, K3, P3, K1, P3, K6, P3, K1, P3, K0(0:3), P0(0:1).
ROW 2 K0(0:1), P0(0:3), K3, P1, K3, P6, K3, P1, K3, P3, K3, P1, K3, P6, K3, P1, K3, P0(0:3), K0(0:1).
ROW 3 As row 1.
ROW 4 K7(7:11), P6, K17, P6, K7(7:11).
Cont in patt as set, working as back, inc one st each end of next, then every foll 3rd(3rd:4th) row to 49(61:63) sts, then on every foll 5th(4th:5th) row to 69(77:85) sts, working inc sts into patt.
Work straight until sleeve measures 19(23:28)cm [7½(9:11)in], ending wrong side row. Place a marker each end of last row. Work another 8(10:12) rows. Bind off.

COLLAR
Join shoulder seams.
With 2¾mm (size 2) set of 4 needles and right side facing, pick up 36(41:46) sts up right front neck, K back neck sts inc 2 sts, pick up 36(41:46) sts down left front neck. 110(122:134) sts. Turn.
Beg alt rows K2, work in P2, K2 rib until row ends fit across bound-off sts at center front neck.
With a 3¼mm (size 3) needle, bind off in rib.

TO MAKE UP
Set in sleeves, sewing row ends above markers to bound-off sts at underarms. Join side and sleeve seams. Lapping right collar over left for a girl and left collar over right for a boy, sew row ends of collar to bound-off sts at center front neck.

•

THE PATTERN FOR ASHLEY'S YELLOW PULLOVER IS ON PAGE 29. JAMIE'S VEST PATTERN IS GIVEN HERE

Jamie's Vest

MEASUREMENTS
To fit approx age 6 mths (2 yrs:4 yrs).
Actual chest measurement 45.5(56:61)cm [18(22:24)in].
Length 23.5(29:33)cm [9¼(1½:13)in] from top of shoulder to bottom of back.

MATERIALS
Rowan Lightweight Double Knitting 25g hanks; 6(7:8) hanks.
1 pair each of 2¾mm (size 2) and 3¼mm (size 3) knitting needles.
Cable needle.
4(5:5) buttons.

GAUGE
26 sts and 34 rows to 10cm (4in) square over st st on 3¼mm (size 3) needles.
34 sts and 40 rows to 10cm (4in) square over patt (slightly stretched) on 3¼mm (size 3) needles.

SPECIAL ABBREVIATIONS
C6B = sl next 3 sts onto cable needle and leave at back of work, K3, then K3 from cable needle.
kw = knitwise.
pw = purlwise.

Note If binding off over a cable, [work 2 tog] 3 times, while binding off in usual way.

LEFT FRONT PATTERN
[35(43:48) sts].
ROW 1 (right side) P0(0:1), K0(0:3), P0(2:3), K0(1:1), P1(3:3), K3, P3, K1, P3, K6, P3, K1, P3, K3, P3, K1, P3, K1(3:3), P0(1:1).
ROW 2 K and P sts as they appear.
ROW 3 As row 1.
ROW 4 K18(21:21), P6, K11(16:21).
ROW 5 As row 1, but work C6B over the K6 sts.
ROW 6 As row 2.
ROWS 7 AND 8 As rows 1 and 4.
These 8 rows form the pattern.

RIGHT FRONT PATTERN
[35(43:48) sts].
ROW 1 (right side) P0(1:1), K1(3:3), P3, K1, P3, K3, P3, K1, P3, K6, P3, K1, P3, K3, P1(3:3), K0(1:1), P0(2:3), K0(0:3), P0(0:1).
ROW 2 K and P sts as they appear.
ROW 3 As row 1.
ROW 4 K11(16:21), P6, K18(21:21).
ROW 5 As row 1, but work C6B over the K6 sts.
ROW 6 As row 2.
ROWS 7 AND 8 As rows 1 and 4.
These 8 rows form the pattern.

BACK

With 2¾mm (size 2) needles cast on 58(72:78) sts.
ROW 1 (right side) [K1, P1] to end.
ROW 2 [P1, K1] to end.
Rep these 2 rows of seed st patt for 1.5cm(½in).
Change to 3¼mm (size 3) needles.
Cont in seed st patt until waistband measures 2cm
(¾in), ending wrong side row.
Beg K row, work in st st until back measures
13.5(18:20.5)cm [5¼(7:8)in], ending P row.

Shape armholes. Bind off 2(3:4) sts at beg of next 2
rows. Dec one st each end of every row to 42(52:58)
sts. Work straight until armholes measure
10(11.5:12.5)cm [4(4½:5)in], ending P row.

Shape shoulders. Bind off 4(6:7) sts at beg of next 4
rows. Bind off rem 26(28:30)sts.

LEFT FRONT

With 3¼mm (size 3) needles cast on 3 sts.
NEXT ROW (right side) K3.
NEXT ROW Inc kw in first st, K2.
NEXT ROW Cast on 5 sts and work as follows: P1, K1,
P3, K3, inc pw in last st.
NEXT ROW Inc kw in first st, K1, P3, K3, P1, K1.
NEXT ROW Cast on 5 sts and work as follows: K3, P3,
K1, P3, K3, P2, inc pw in last st.
NEXT ROW Inc kw in first st, K13, P3.
NEXT ROW Cast on 5 sts and work as follows: P2, K6,
P3, K1, P3, K3, P3, K1, inc pw in last st.
NEXT ROW Inc kw in first st, K1, P1, K3, P3, K3, P1,
K3, P6, K2.
NEXT ROW Cast on 5 sts and work as follows: P3, K1,
P3, K6, P3, K1, P3, K3, P3, K1, P2, inc pw in last st.
NEXT ROW Inc kw in first 0(1:1) st, K18(17:17), P6, K7.
NEXT ROW Cast on 4(5:5) sts and work as follows:
P1(2:2), K3, P3, K1, P3, C6B, P3, K1, P3, K3, P3,
K1, P3, K1, inc pw in last 0(1:1) st.
NEXT ROW Inc pw in first 0(1:1) st, P1(2:2), K3, P1,
K3, P3, K3, P1, K3, P6, K3, P1, K3, P3, K1(2:2).
NEXT ROW Cast on 0(4:5) sts and work as follows:
P0(2:3), K0(1:1), P1(3:3), K3, P3, K1, P3, K6, P3,
K1, P3, K3, P3, K1, P3, K1(3:3), P0(1:1).
NEXT ROW K18(21:21), P6, K11(16:17).
NEXT ROW Cast on 0(0:4) sts and work as follows:
P0(0:1), K0(0:3), P0(2:3), K0(1:1), P1(3:3), K3, P3,
K1, P3, K6, P3, K1, P3, K3, P3, K1, P3, K1(3:3),
P0(1:1). 35(43:48) sts.
The last row was row 1 of pattern (see previous page).
Cont as set until straight edge of left front side seam
measures same as st st part of back to beg of armhole
shaping, ending at side edge.

Shape armhole and front neck. Keeping patt
correct, bind off 3(4:5) sts at beg of next row.
Work 1 row (omit this row when working right front).
Dec one st at front edge on next and every foll alt row,
AT THE SAME TIME, dec one st at armhole edge on
every row to 23(28:32) sts.

Keeping armhole edge straight, cont to dec at front
edge on every foll alt row from last dec to 12(21:27)
sts, then on every foll 3rd row to 10(15:18) sts.
Work a few rows straight until front measures same as
back to beg of shoulder shaping, ending armhole edge.

Shape shoulder. Bind off 5(8:9) sts at beg of next
row. Work 1 row. Bind off.

RIGHT FRONT

With 3¼mm (size 3) needles cast on 3 sts.
NEXT ROW (right side) K3.
NEXT ROW K2, inc kw in last st.
NEXT ROW Inc pw in first st, K3.
NEXT ROW Bind on 5 sts and work as follows: K1, P1,
K3, P3, K1, inc kw in last st.
NEXT ROW Inc pw in first st, P2, K3, P3, K1, P1.
NEXT ROW Bind on 5 sts and work as follows: P3, K13,
inc kw in last st.
NEXT ROW Inc pw in first st, K1, P3, K3, P3, K1, P3,
K3.
NEXT ROW Bind on 5 sts and work as follows: K2, P6,
K3, P1, K3, P3, K3, P1, K1, inc kw in last st.
NEXT ROW Inc pw in first st, P2, K1, P3, K3, P3, K1,
P3, K6, P2.
NEXT ROW Bind on 5 sts and work as follows: K7, P6,
K18(17:17), inc kw in last 0(1:1) st.
Cont as set to match left front, reversing shaping and
noting exception in parentheses.

FRONT BOTTOM EDGING AND BUTTON BAND

With 2¾mm (size 2) needles cast on 6 sts.
Work in seed st patt as given for back waistband until
band, slightly stretched, measures from side seam of
front to inner edge of point, ending outer edge of band.
Work mitered corner as follows:
*** NEXT 2 ROWS** Patt 2, turn, sl 1, patt 1.
NEXT 2 ROWS Patt 3, turn, sl 1, patt to end.
NEXT 2 ROWS Patt 4, turn, sl 1, patt to end.
NEXT 2 ROWS Patt 5, turn, sl 1, patt to end *.
Work straight across all sts until band, slightly
stretched, measures from point to beg of straight edge
of front, ending outer edge.
Rep from * to * for 2nd mitered corner.
Work straight across all sts until band, slightly
stretched, fits up front edge to beg of neck shaping,
ending at inner edge.

Shape lapel. Inc one st at inner edge on next and
every foll alt row to 11(11:13) sts, working inc sts in
patt.
Work straight until lapel measures 6.5(7.5:8)cm
[2½(3:3¼)in] from beg of incs, ending at straight edge.
Bind off in patt. Sew edging and band in place.
Place markers on band for 4(5:5) buttons, first at top of
2nd mitered corner, last at beg of lapel (neck) shaping
and rem evenly spaced between.

FRONT BOTTOM EDGING AND BUTTONHOLE BAND
Work as given for front bottom edging and button band reversing shaping and making buttonholes to match markers as follows:
BUTTONHOLE ROW 1 (right side) Patt 2, bind off 2, patt to end.
BUTTONHOLE ROW 2 Patt, binding on 2 sts over those bound off.

COLLAR
With 2¾mm (size 2) needles cast on 24(26:28) sts.
Working in seed st as given for back waistband and keeping patt correct, bind on 5(5:6) sts at beg of next 4 rows, then 5 sts at beg of foll 2 rows, working inc sts in patt. 54(56:62) sts.
Cont straight in patt until straight edge of row ends measure 5(5:5.5)cm [2(2:2¼)in]. Bind off loosely in patt.

ARMHOLE BANDS
Join shoulder seams.
With 2¼mm (size 2) needles and right side facing, pick up 70(80:86) sts around armhole edge.
Work in seed st patt as given for back waistband for 1.5cm (½in), dec one st each end of every row. Bind off in patt.

TO MAKE UP
Sew cast-on edge of collar to back neck, beginning and ending at top of front bands, then join bound-off edge of front bands to row ends of collar for 2(2:2.5)cm [¾(¾:1)in] from inner edge, leaving remainder free.
Join side and armhole band seams, matching front bands to back waistband. Sew on buttons.

Chelsea's Jacket
Shown on page 34

MEASUREMENTS
To fit approx age 6 mths (2 yrs:4 yrs).
Actual chest measurement 50(61:66)cm [19¾(24:26)in].
Length 25.5(31.5:35.5)cm [10(12½:14)in].
Sleeve seam 19(23:28)cm [7½(9:11)in].

MATERIALS
Rowan Lightweight Double Knitting 25g hanks; 7(8:9) hanks.
1 pair each of 2¾mm (size 2) and 3¼mm (size 3) knitting needles.
Cable needle.
4(5:5) small buttons.

GAUGE
34 sts and 40 rows to 10cm (4in) square over patt (slightly stretched) on 3¼mm (size 3) needles.

SPECIAL ABBREVIATION
C6B = sl next 3 sts onto cable needle and leave at back of work, K3, then K3 from cable needle.

Note If binding off over a cable, [work 2 tog] 3 times, while binding off in usual way.

BACK
With 2¾mm (size 2) needles cast on 54(66:78) sts.
RIB ROW 1 (right side) K2, * P2, K2; rep from * to end.
RIB ROW 2 P2, * K2, P2; rep from * to end.
Cont in rib until waistband measures 4(5:5)cm [1½(2:2)in], ending rib row 2 and inc to 84(102:110) sts in last row.
Change to 3¼mm (size 3) needles.
Work in patt as follows:
ROW 1 (right side) P2(0:0), K1(0:0), P3(0:0), K3(0:0), P3(0:2), K1(0:1), P3(2:3), * K6, P3, K1, P3, K3, P3, K1, P3; rep from * to last 22(8:12) sts, K6, P3(2:3), K1(0:1), P3(0:2), K3(0:0), P3(0:0), K1(0:0), P2(0:0).
ROW 2 K2(0:0), P1(0:0), K3(0:0), P3(0:0), K3(0:2), P1(0:1), K3(2:3), * P6, K3, P1, K3, P3, K3, P1, K3; rep from * to last 22(8:12) sts, P6, K3(2:3), P1(0:1), K3(0:2), P3(0:0), K3(0:0), P1(0:0), K2(0:0).
ROW 3 As row 1.
ROW 4 K16(2:6), * P6, K17; rep from * to last 22(8:12) sts, P6, K16(2:6).
ROW 5 P2(0:0), K1(0:0), P3(0:0), K3(0:0), P3(0:2), K1(0:1), P3(2:3), * C6B, P3, K1, P3, K3, P3, K1, P3; rep from * to last 22(8:12) sts, C6B, P3(2:3), K1(0:1), P3(0:2), K3(0:0), P3(0:0), K1(0:0), P2(0:0).
ROW 6 As row 2.
ROWS 7 AND 8 As rows 1 and 4.
These 8 rows form the patt.
Cont in patt until back measures 15(20.5:23)cm [6(8:9)in], ending wrong side row.

Shape armholes. Keeping patt correct, bind off 7(10:12) sts at beg of next 2 rows. 70(82:86) sts.
Work straight until armholes measure 10(11.5:12.5)cm [4(4½:5)in], ending wrong side row.

Shape shoulders. Bind off 17(22:23) sts at beg of next 2 rows. Bind off.

LEFT FRONT
With 2¾mm (size 2) needles cast on 26(30:34) sts.
Work in rib as back for 4(5:5)cm [1½(2:2)in], ending rib row 2 and inc to 39(48:52) sts in last row.
Change to 3¼mm (size 3) needles.
Work in patt as follows:
ROW 1 (right side) P2(0:0), K1(0:0), P3(0:0), K3(0:0), P3(0:2), K1(0:1), P3(2:3), * K6, P3, K1, P3, K3, P3, K1, P3; rep from * once(twice:twice).
ROW 2 * K3, P1, K3, P3, K3, P1, K3, K6; rep from * once(twice:twice), K3(2:3), P1(0:1), K3(0:2), P3(0:0), K3(0:0), P1(0:0), K2(0:0).
Cont in patt as set, working as back, until front measures same as back to beg of armhole shaping, ending wrong side row (for right front end right side row here).

Shape armhole. Keeping patt correct, bind off 7(10:12) sts at beg of next row.
Work 1 row (for right front omit this row). 32(38:40) sts.

Shape neck. Dec one st at neck edge on next and 10(9:8) foll alt rows, then on every foll 3rd row to 17(22:23) sts.
Work a few rows straight until front measures same as back to shoulder, ending armhole edge. Bind off.

RIGHT FRONT
Work as given for left front, placing patt as follows:
ROW 1 (right side) * P3, K1, P3, K3, P3, K1, P3, K6; rep from * once(twice:twice), P3(2:3), K1(0:1), P3(0:2), K3(0:0), P3(0:0), K1(0:0), P2(0:0).
ROW 2 K2(0:0), P1(0:0), K3(0:0), P3(0:0), K3(0:2), P1(0:1), K3(2:3), * P6, K3, P1, K3, P3, K3, P1, K3; rep from * once(twice:twice).
Complete as left front noting exceptions in parentheses.

SLEEVES
With 2³/₄mm (size 2) needles cast on 32(32:36) sts.
Work in K2, P2 rib for 4(5:5)cm [1¹/₂(2:2)in], inc to 45(45:53) sts in last row.
Change to 3¹/₄mm (size 3) needles.
Work in patt as follows:
ROW 1 (right side) P0(0:2), K1(1:3), P3, K1, P3, K6, P3, K1, P3, K3, P3, K1, P3, K6, P3, K1, P3, K1(1:3), P0(0:2).
ROW 2 K0(0:2), P1(1:3), K3, P1, K3, P6, K3, P1, K3, P3, K3, P1, K3, P6, K3, P1, K3, P1(1:3), K0(0:2).
ROW 3 As row 1.
ROW 4 K8(8:12), P6, K17, P6, K8(8:12).
Cont in patt as set, working as back, inc one st each end of next and every foll 3rd(3rd:4th) row to 49(61:63) sts, then on every foll 5th(4th:5th) row to 71(79:87) sts, working inc sts in patt.
Work straight until sleeve measures 19(23:28)cm [7¹/₂(9:11)in], ending wrong side row. Place a marker each end of last row. Work another 10(12:14) rows. Bind off.

BUTTON BAND AND COLLAR
Join shoulder seams.
With 2³/₄mm (size 2) needles cast on 10(14:14) sts.
Beg alt rows P2, work in K2, P2 rib until band, slightly stretched, fits up front to beg of neck shaping, ending wrong side row (for buttonhole band end right side row here).

Shape collar. Keeping rib correct, inc one st at beg (inside edge) of next and every foll alt row to 28(34:38) sts.

•

CABLES AND A SHAWL COLLAR GIVE CHELSEA'S
JACKET A VERY SPECIAL LOOK

Work straight until collar, when slightly stretched, reaches to center back neck. Bind off in rib.
Mark positions on band for 4(5:5) buttons, the first approx 1.5cm (¹/₂in) from beg, last at beg of collar and rem evenly spaced between.

BUTTONHOLE BAND AND COLLAR
Work as given for button band and collar, noting exception in parentheses and making buttonholes to match markers as follows:
BUTTONHOLE ROW 1 (right side) Rib 4(6:6), bind off 2, rib to end.
BUTTONHOLE ROW 2 Rib, casting on 2 sts over those bound off.

TO MAKE UP
Set in sleeves, sewing row ends above markers to bound-off sts at underarms. Join side and sleeve seams. Sew front bands and shaped edge of collar in place, then join bound-off edges of collar together at center back neck. Sew on buttons.

BOBBLES

MAKING BOBBLES IS a technique for the slightly more experienced knitter, but it is very satisfying to do, and the bobbles certainly add an exciting variety of textures to a child's pullover. Ashley's pullover, shown here, is ideal for cold days for both boys and girls. Antonia's and Laura's pullovers, shown on pages 40 and 43, are for occasions when girls want to look especially pretty. The designs given here use different yarns, including luxurious but washable wool and silk, so there is something for all seasons.

Ashley's Pullover

Shown on page 37

M E A S U R E M E N T S

To fit approx age 6 mths (2 yrs:4 yrs).
Actual chest measurement 48(58.5:63.5)cm
[19(23:25)in].
Length 25.5(31.5:35.5)cm [10(12½:14)in].
Sleeve seam 19(23:28)cm [7½(9:11)in].

M A T E R I A L S

Rowan Lightweight Double Knitting 25g hanks,
10(11:12) hanks.
1 pair each of 2¾mm (size 2) and 3¼mm (size 3)
knitting needles. Cable needle.

G A U G E

35 sts and 38 rows to 10cm (4in) square over patt on
3¼mm (size 3) needles.

S P E C I A L   A B B R E V I A T I O N S

C4B = sl next 2 sts onto cable needle and leave at back
of work, K2, then K2 from cable needle.
C4F = sl next 2 sts onto cable needle and leave at front
of work, K2, then K2 from cable needle.
MB = [K into front, back, front and back] of next st,
turn, P4, turn, K4, turn, P4, turn, sl 1, K1, psso, K2
tog, then pass 2nd st over first st.

PATT PANEL 1 (3 sts)
ROW 1 (right side) K1, P1, K1.
ROW 2 P3.

PATT PANEL 2 (9 sts)
ROW 1 (right side) P4, K1, P4.
ROW 2 K4, P1, K4.
ROW 3 P3, K1, P1, K1, P3.
ROW 4 K3, P1, K1, P1, K3.
ROW 5 P2, [K1, P1] twice, K1, P2.
ROW 6 K2, [P1, K1] twice, P1, K2.
ROW 7 P1, [K1, P1] 4 times.
ROW 8 K1, [P1, K1] 4 times.
ROW 9 P2, [K1, P1] twice, K2, P2.
ROW 10 K2, [P1, K1] twice, P1, K2.
ROW 11 P3, K1, P1, K1, P3.
ROW 12 K3, P1, K1, P1, K3.

PATT PANEL 3 (13 sts)
ROW 1 (right side) P2, K9, P2.
ROW 2 K2, P9, K2.
ROW 3 P2, K9, P2.
ROW 4 K2, P9, K2.
ROW 5 P2, C4B, K1, C4F, P2.
ROW 6 K2, P9, K2.
ROW 7 P2, K4, MB, K4, P2.
ROW 8 K2, K9, K2.
ROW 9 P2, K2, MB, K3, MB, K2, P2.
ROW 10 K2, P9, K2.
ROW 11 P2, C4B, K1, C4F, P2.
ROW 12 K2, P9, K2.

B A C K

With 2¾mm (size 2) needles cast on 54(68:74) sts.
Work in K1, P1 rib for 4(5:5)cm [1½(2:2)in] inc to
83(101:109) sts in last row.
Change to 3¼mm (size 3) needles.
Work in patt as follows:
ROW 1 (right side) Work row 1 of patt panels as follows:
P0(0:1), K1, panel 1 twice(once:twice), panel 0(2:2),
panel 0(1:1), panel 3, * panel 1, panel 2, panel 1, panel
3; rep from * to last 7(16:20) sts, panel 0(1:1), panel
0(2:2), panel 1 twice(once:twice), K1, P0(0:1).
ROW 2 Work row 2 of patt panels as follows: P1(1:2),
panel 1 twice(once:twice), panel 0(2:2), panel 0(1:1),
panel 3, * panel 1, panel 2, panel 1, panel 3; rep from *
to last 7(16:20) sts, panel 0(1:1), panel 0(2:2), panel 1
twice(once:twice), P1(1:2).
These 2 rows set the patt.
Cont in patt as set repeating the various patt panel rows
as required until back measures 25.5(31.5:35.5)cm
[10(12½:14)in], ending wrong side row.

Shape shoulders. Keeping patt correct, bind off
8(11:12) sts at beg of next 2 rows, 8(10:11) sts at beg
of foll 2 rows, then 7(10:11) sts at beg of next 2 rows.
Leave rem sts on a holder.

F R O N T

Work as given for back until front measures 8(8:10)
rows **less** than back to beg of shoulder shaping, ending
wrong side row.

Shape neck. NEXT ROW Patt 35(43:47), turn and leave
rem sts on a spare needle.
Keeping patt correct, bind off 4 sts at neck edge on
next and foll alt row. Dec one st at neck edge on every
row to 23(31:34) sts.
Work 0(0:1) row straight, ending side edge.

Shape shoulder. Bind off 8(11:12) sts at beg of next
row, then 8(10:11) sts at beg of foll alt row.
Work 1 row. Bind off.
With right side facing, sl center 13(15:15) sts on a
holder, join yarn to rem sts and patt to end. Work 1
row. Complete to match first side.

S L E E V E S

With 2¾mm (size 2) needles cast on 32(34:40) sts.
Work in K1, P1, rib for 4(5:5)cm [1½(2:2)in] inc to
43(43:51) sts in last row.
Change to 3¼mm (size 3) needles.
Work in patt as follows:
ROW 1 (right side) Work row 1 of patt panels as follows:
K0(0:2), P0(0:2), panel 1, panel 2, panel 1, panel 3,
panel 1, panel 2, panel 1, P0(0:2), K0(0:2).
ROW 2 Work row 2 of patt panels as follows: P0(0:2),
K0(0:2), panel 1, panel 2, panel 1, panel 3, panel 1,
panel 2, panel 1, K0(0:2), P0(0:2).
These 2 rows set the patt.
Cont in patt as set, working as back, AT THE SAME
TIME, inc one st each end of next and every foll

3rd(3rd:4th) row to 53(65:79) sts, then on every foll 4th(4th:5th) row to 69(77:87) sts, working inc sts in patt.
Work straight until sleeve measures 19(23:28)cm [7$\frac{1}{2}$(9:11)in], ending wrong side row. Bind off.

NECKBAND

Join right shoulder seam.
With 2$\frac{3}{4}$mm (size 2) needles and right side facing, pick up 15(17:19) sts down left front neck, K front neck sts, pick up 15(17:19) sts up right front neck, then K back neck sts. 80(88:94) sts.
Work in K1, P1 rib for 1.5cm ($\frac{1}{2}$in).
With 3$\frac{1}{4}$mm (size 3) needles, bind off in rib.

TO MAKE UP

Join left shoulder and neckband seam. Sew in sleeves, placing center of bound-off edges at shoulder seams.
Join side and sleeve seams.

Antonia's Pullover

MEASUREMENTS

To fit approx age 6 mths (2 yrs:4 yrs).
Actual chest measurement 48(58.5:63.5)cm [19(23:25)in].
Length 25.5(31.5:35.5)cm [10(12$\frac{1}{2}$:14)in].
Sleeve seam 19(23:28)cm [7$\frac{1}{2}$(9:11)in].

MATERIALS

Rowan's Edina Ronay Silk and Wool 20g balls;
10(12:13) balls.
1 pair each of 2$\frac{1}{4}$mm (size 1) and 3mm (size 2) knitting needles.
crochet hook.
2 buttons.

GAUGE

30 sts and 40 rows to 10cm (4in) square over patt on 3mm (size 2) needles.

SPECIAL ABBREVIATION

MB = [K into front, back, front, back and front] of next st, turn, P5, turn, K5, turn, P5, turn, sl 1, K1, psso, sl 1, K2 tog, pass 2nd and 3rd sts over first st.

BACK

With 2$\frac{1}{4}$mm (size 1) needles cast on 62(78:82) sts.
Beg alt rows P2, work in K2, P2 rib for 4(5:5)cm [1$\frac{1}{2}$(2:2)in], ending wrong side row and inc to 71(87:95) sts in last row.
Change to 3mm (size 2) needles.
Beg K row, work 4 rows in st st.
Work in patt as follows:
ROW 1 (right side) K11(7:11), MB, * K11, MB; rep from * to last 11(7:11) sts, K to end.
ROW 2 P.
ROW 3 K.
ROW 4 P.
ROW 5 K9(5:9), MB, K3, MB, * K7, MB, K3, MB; rep from * to last 9(5:9) sts, K to end.
ROWS 6 TO 8 As rows 2 to 4.
ROW 9 K7(3:7), MB, K7, MB, * K3, MB, K7, MB; rep from * to last 7(3:7) sts, K to end.
ROWS 10 TO 12 As rows 2 to 4.
ROW 13 K5(1:5), MB, * K11, MB; rep from * to last 5(1:5) sts, K to end.
ROWS 14 TO 24 Reverse patt by working row 12 back to row 2 in this order.
These 24 rows form the patt.
Cont in patt until back measures 25.5(31.5:35.5)cm [10(12$\frac{1}{2}$:14)in], ending wrong side row.

Shape shoulders. Keeping patt correct, bind off 7(9:11) sts at beg of next 2 rows, 7(9:10) sts at beg of foll 2 rows, then 6(8:9) sts at beg of next 2 rows.
Leave rem sts on a holder.

FRONT

Work as given for back until front measures 8(8:10) rows **less** than back to beg of shoulder shaping, ending wrong side row.

Shape neck. NEXT ROW Patt 29(36:40), turn and leave rem sts on a spare needle.
Keeping patt correct, bind off 3 sts at neck edge on next row, then 2(3:3) sts on foll alt row. Dec one st at neck edge on every row to 20(26:30) sts.
Work 0(0:2) rows straight, ending side edge.

Shape shoulder. Bind off 7(9:11) sts at beg of next

row, then 7(9:10) sts on foll alt row. Work 1 row. Bind off.
With right side facing sl center 13(15:15) sts on a holder, join yarn to rem sts and patt to end.
Work 1 row. Complete to match first side.

SLEEVES

With 2¼mm (size 1) needles cast on 34(38:46) sts.
Beg alt rows P2, work in K2, P2 rib for 4(5:5)cm [1½(2:2)in], ending wrong side row and inc to 35(41:47) sts in last row.
Change to 3mm (size 2) needles.
Beg K row, work 4 rows in st st, inc one st each end of 4th row. 37(43:49) sts.
Work in patt as follows:
ROW 1 (right side) K6(9:12), MB, * K11, MB; rep from * to last 6(9:12) sts, K to end.
ROW 2 P.
ROW 3 K.
ROW 4 P, but inc one st each end of row on **1st and 2nd sizes only**.
ROW 5 K0(0:2), 0(0:MB), K5(8:7), MB, K3, MB, * K7, MB, K3, MB; rep from * to last 5(8:10) sts, K5(8:7), 0(0:MB), K0(0:2).
Cont in patt as set, working as back and inc one st each end of every 5th(5th:6th) row from last inc to 57(55:75) sts, then on **2nd size only** on every 4th row to 69 sts, working inc sts in patt on **all sizes**.
Cont straight until sleeve measures 19(23:28)cm [7½(9:11)in], ending wrong side row. Bind off.

NECKBAND

Join right shoulder seam.
With 2¼mm (size 1) needles and right side facing, pick up 13(13:14) sts down left front neck, K front neck sts inc 1(0:1) st, pick up 13(13:14) sts up right front neck, then K back neck sts inc 3(2:3) sts. 74(78:82) sts.
Beg alt rows P2, work in K2, P2 rib for 1.5cm (½in).
With 3mm (size 2) needles, bind off in rib.

TO MAKE UP

Join left shoulder seam for 3(5:5.5)cm [1¼(2:2¼)in], leaving remainder of shoulder and neckband open. Sew on sleeves, placing center of bound-off edge of sleeves at shoulder seams. Join side and sleeve seams. Crochet a row of slip stitch around shoulder opening, then another row of slip stitch along front edge only, working 2 button loops. Sew buttons on back edge to match.

•

LITTLE GIRLS LIKE ANTONIA LOOK ESPECIALLY
PRETTY IN FASHIONABLE STRONG COLORS

Laura's Pullover

Shown on page 43, left

MEASUREMENTS

To fit approx age 6 mths (2 yrs:4 yrs).
Actual chest measurement 48(58.5:63.5)cm [19(23:25)in].
Length 25.5(31.5:35.5)cm [10(12½:14)in].
Sleeve seam 19(23:28)cm [7½(9:11)in].

MATERIALS

Rowan's Edina Ronay Silk and Wool 20g balls; 10(12:13) balls.
1 pair each of 2mm (size 0) and 2¾mm (size 2) knitting needles.

GAUGE

37 sts and 46½ rows to 10cm (4in) square over patt on 2¾mm (size 2) needles.

SPECIAL ABBREVIATION

MB = [K1, P1, K1 and P1] all into next st.

Note When working in patt, stitches are increased on row 3, then decreased on row 6. These sts are not included in stitch counts; when shaping count each bobble as one st.

BACK

With 2mm (size 0) needles cast on 78(96:104) sts.
Work in K1, P1 rib for 4(5:5)cm [1½(2:2)in] inc to 88(106:116) sts in last row.
Change to 2¾mm (size 2) needles.
Work in patt as follows:
ROW 1 (right side) P3(4:5), K2, * P6, K2; rep from * to last 3(4:5) sts, P3(4:5).
ROW 2 K3(4:5), P2, * K6, P2; rep from * to last 3(4:5) sts, K3(4:5).
ROW 3 P3(4:5), MB, MB, * P6, MB, MB; rep from * to last 3(4:5) sts, P3(4:5).
ROW 4 K.
ROW 5 P.
ROW 6 K3(4:5), P4 tog, P4 tog, * K6, P4 tog, P4 tog; rep from * to last 3(4:5) sts, K3(4:5).
These 6 rows form the pattern.
Cont in patt until back measures 15(20.5:23)cm [6(8:9)in], ending wrong side row.

Shape armholes. Keeping patt correct, bind off 4(5:5) sts at beg of next 2 rows. Dec one st each end of next 3(3:5) rows, then 2(3:2) foll alt rows. 70(84:92) sts.
Work straight until armholes measure 10(11.5:12.5) cm [4(4½:5)in], ending wrong side row.

Shape shoulders. Bind off 5(7:8) sts at beg of next 6 rows. Leave rem sts on a holder.

FRONT

Work as given for back until front measures 12(12:14)

rows **less** than back to beg off shoulder shaping ending wrong side row. 70(84:92) sts.

Shape neck. NEXT ROW Patt 28(34:38), turn and leave rem sts on a spare needle.
Keeping patt correct, bind off 4 sts at neck edge on next row, then 3 sts on foll alt row. Dec one st at neck edge on next 6(6:7) rows. 15(21:24) sts.
Work 2(2:3) rows straight, ending armhole edge.

Shape shoulder. Bind off 5(7:8) sts at beg of next and foll alt row. Work 1 row. Bind off.
With right side facing sl center 14(16:16) sts on a holder, join yarn to rem sts and patt to end.
Work 1 row. Complete to match first side.

S L E E V E S
With 2mm (size 0) needles cast on 48(48:56) sts.
Work in K1, P1 rib for 4(5:5)cm [1½(2:2)in].
Change to 2¾mm (size 2) needles.
Work in patt as follows:
ROW 1 (right side) P3, K2, * P6, K2; rep from * to last 3 sts, P3.
ROW 2 K3, P2, * K6, P2; rep from * to last 3 sts, K3.
Cont in patt as set, working as back and inc one st each end of 3rd(next:next), then 7(7:17) foll 6th(3rd:5th) rows, then on **2nd size only** on 10 foll 4th rows, working inc sts in patt on **all sizes**. 64(84:92) sts.
Cont straight until sleeve measures approx 19(23:28)cm [7½(9:11)in], ending wrong side row and same patt row as back to beg of armhole shaping.

Shape sleeve top. Keeping patt correct, bind off 4(5:5) sts at beg of next 2 rows. Dec one st each end of next 3(5:5) rows, then 7(5:6) foll alt rows, then foll 4(9:12) rows. 28(36:36) sts.
Bind off 2(3:3) sts at beg of next 2 rows, then 3(4:4) sts at beg of foll 4 rows. Bind off.

N E C K B A N D
Join right shoulder seam.
With 2mm (size 0) needles and right side facing, pick up 21(22:24) sts down left front neck, K front neck sts inc 3 sts, pick up 21(22:24) sts up right front neck, then K back neck sts inc 5 sts. 104(110:116) sts.
Work in K1, P1 rib for 1.5cm (½in). With 2¾mm (size 2) needles, bind off in rib.

T O   M A K E   U P
Join left shoulder and neckband seam. Set in sleeves.
Join side and sleeve seams.

Jasmin's Cardigan

M E A S U R E M E N T S
To fit approx age 6 mths (2 yrs:4 yrs).
Actual chest measurement 49(59:64)cm [19¼(23¼:25¼)in].
Length 25.5(31.5:35.5)cm [10(12½:14)in].
Sleeve seam 19(23:28)cm [7½(9:11)in].

M A T E R I A L S
Rowan's Edina Ronay Silk and Wool 20g balls; 10(12:13) balls.
1 pair each of 2mm (size 0) and 2¾mm (size 2) knitting needles.
6(7:7) small buttons.

G A U G E
37 sts and 46½ rows to 10cm (4in) square over patt on 2¾mm (size 2) needles.

S P E C I A L   A B B R E V I A T I O N
MB = [K1, P1, K1 and P1] all into next st.

Note When working in patt, stitches are increased on row 3, then decreased on row 6. These sts are not included in stitch counts; when shaping count each bobble as one st.

B A C K
Work as given for back of Laura's pullover (page 41).

L E F T   F R O N T
With 2mm (size 0) needles cast on 38(46:50) sts.
Work in K1, P1 rib for 4(5:5)cm [1½(2:2)in] inc to 42(51:56) sts in last row.
Change to 2¾mm (size 2) needles.
Work in patt as follows:
ROW 1 (right side) P3(4:5), K2, * P6, K2; rep from * to last 5(5:1) sts, P5(5:1).
ROW 2 K5(5:1), P2, * K6, P2; rep from * to last 3(4:5) sts, K3(4:5).
ROW 3 P3(4:5), MB, MB, * P6, MB, MB; rep from * to last 5(5:1) sts, P5(5:1).
ROW 4 K.
ROW 5 P.
ROW 6 K5(5:1), P4 tog, P4 tog, * K6, P4 tog, P4 tog; rep from * to last 3(4:5) sts, K3(4:5).
These 6 rows form the pattern.
Cont in patt until front measures same as back to beg of armhole shaping, ending wrong side row (for right front end right side row here).

Shape armhole and front neck. Keeping patt correct, bind off 4(5:5) sts at beg of next row.
Work 1 row (for right front omit this row).
Dec one st at neck edge on next and 3(4:4) foll alt rows, AT THE SAME TIME, dec one st at armhole edge on next 3(3:5) rows, then 2(3:2) foll alt rows. 29(35:39) sts.
Keeping armhole edge straight, dec one st at neck edge

LAURA AND JASMIN WEAR A PULLOVER AND CARDIGAN WORKED IN THE SAME BOBBLE PATTERN

•

on 7(2:2) foll alt rows, then every foll 3rd row to
15(21:24) sts.
Work a few rows straight until front measures same as
back to beg of shoulder shaping, ending armhole edge.

Shape shoulder. Bind off 5(7:8) sts at beg of next and
foll alt row. Work 1 row. Bind off.

RIGHT FRONT
Work as given for left front, noting exceptions in
parentheses and placing patt as follows:
ROW 1 (right side) P5(5:1), K2, * P6, K2; rep from * to
last 3(4:5) sts, P3(4:5).
ROW 2 K3(4:5), P2, * K6, P2; rep from * to last 5(5:1)
sts, K5(5:1).

SLEEVES
Work as given for sleeves of Laura's pullover (page 41).

BUTTON BAND
Join shoulder seams.

With 2mm (size 0) needles cast on 11 sts.
Beg alt rows P1, work in K1, P1 rib until band, slightly
stretched, fits up left front and across to center back
neck. Bind off in rib.
Sew band in place. Mark positions on band for 6(7:7)
buttons, first approx 1.5cm ($\frac{1}{2}$in) from bind-on edge,
last at beg of neck shaping and rem evenly spaced
between.

BUTTONHOLE BAND
Work as given for button band making buttonholes to
match markers as follows:
BUTTONHOLE ROW 1 (right side) Rib 4, bind off 3, rib to
end.
BUTTONHOLE ROW 2 Rib, casting on 3 sts over those
bound off.

TO MAKE UP
Set in sleeves. Join side and sleeve seams. Join bound-
off edges of front bands together at center back neck.
Sew on buttons.

FAIR ISLE

THESE ARE THE designs on which you can really show off your color knitting skills. Each of the six sweaters in this section has a different Fair Isle pattern, so there are plenty to choose from. All of them are in exciting colors which will team with simple skirts or pants to make an instantly eye-catching outfit. Fair Isle designs have been continuously popular through the decades, but they had a vogue in the thirties, and my designs are based on originals of this period.

Chelsea's Cardigan

Shown on page 45, right

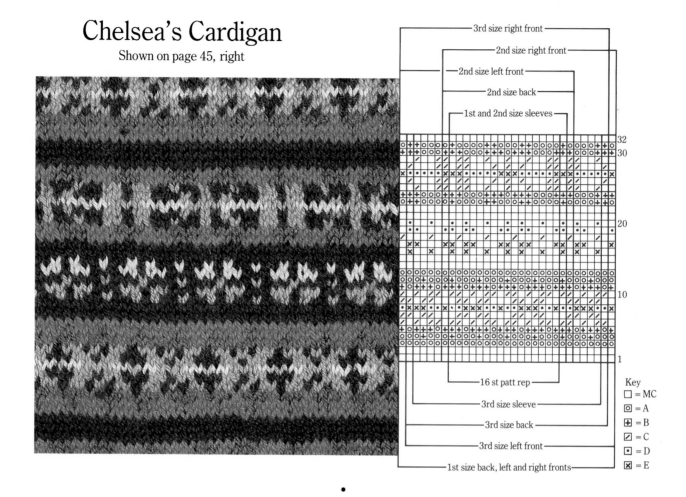

3rd size right front
2nd size right front
2nd size left front
2nd size back
1st and 2nd size sleeves

16 st patt rep
3rd size sleeve
3rd size back
3rd size left front
1st size back, left and right fronts

Key
☐ = MC
⊙ = A
⊞ = B
☑ = C
⊡ = D
☒ = E

•

MEASUREMENTS

To fit approx age 6 mths (2 yrs:4 yrs).
Actual chest measurement 50(60.5:66)cm
[19³/₄(23³/₄:26)in].
Length approx 25.5(31.5:35.5)cm [10(12¹/₂:14)in].
Sleeve seam approx 19(23:28)cm [7¹/₂(9:11)in].

MATERIALS

Rowan 4ply Botany 25g hanks; Main color (MC) Navy
(97) 4(4:6) hanks, 1st contrasting color (A) Deep Pink
(631) 1(2:2) hanks, 2nd contrasting color (B) Green
(39) 1(2:2) hanks, 3rd contrasting color (C) Light Pink
(95) 1(1:1) hank, 4th contrasting color (D) Pale Yellow
(06) 1(1:1) hank, 5th contrasting color (E) Pale Blue
(49) 1(1:1) hank.
1 pair each of 2mm (size 0) and 2³/₄mm (size 2) knitting
needles.
6(6:7) small buttons.

GAUGE

40 sts and 44 rows to 10cm (4in) square over patt on
2³/₄mm (size 2) needles.

Note When working patt from chart strand yarn not in
use loosely across back of work over no more than 3 sts
at a time, making sure that the same gauge is obtained
throughout.

BACK

With 2mm (size 0) needles and MC, cast on 76(94:102)
sts.
Work in K1, P1 rib for 4(5:5)cm [1¹/₂(2:2)in] inc to
95(115:125) sts in last row.
Change to 2³/₄mm (size 2) needles.
Beg K row, work in st st from chart following markers
for back until back measures approx 15(20.5:23)cm
[6(8:9)in], ending patt row 18(2:12).

Shape armholes. Keeping patt correct, bind off 5 sts
at beg of next 2 rows. Dec one st each end of every row
to 79(95:105) sts, then on every foll alt row to
75(89:99) sts.
Work straight until armholes measure approx
10(11.5:12.5)cm [4(4¹/₂:5)in], patt row 30(18:4).

Shape shoulders. Bind off 9(11:13) sts at beg of next
2 rows, then 8(11:12) sts at beg of foll 2 rows. Leave
rem sts on a holder.

LEFT FRONT

With 2mm (size 0) needles and MC, cast on 38(46:50)
sts.
Work in K1, P1 rib for 4(5:5)cm [1¹/₂(2:2)in] inc to
47(57:62) sts in last row.
Change to 2³/₄mm (size 2) needles.

Beg K row, work in st st from chart following markers for left front until front measures same as back to beg of armhole shaping, ending patt row 18(2:12) (for right front end patt row 19[3:13] here).

Shape armhole. Keeping patt correct, bind off 5 sts at beg of next row.
Work 1 row (omit this row when working right front).
Dec one st at armhole edge on every row to 39(47:52) sts, then on every foll alt row to 37(44:49) sts.
Work straight until armhole measures 10(10:12) rows (for right front read 9[9:11] rows here) **less** than back to beg of shoulder shaping, ending at armhole edge.

Shape neck. NEXT ROW Patt 30(36:41), turn and leave rem sts on a holder. Bind off 4 sts at neck edge on next row, then 3(4:4) sts at this edge on foll alt row. Dec one st at neck edge on every row to 17(22:25) sts, ending armhole edge.

Shape shoulder. Bind off 9(11:13) sts at beg of next row. Work 1 row. Bind off.

RIGHT FRONT
Work as given for left front noting exceptions in parentheses and following markers for right front on chart.

SLEEVES
With 2mm (size 0) needles and MC, cast on 44(46:54) sts.
Work in K1, P1 rib for 4(5:5)cm [1½(2:2)in] inc to 49(49:59) sts in last row.
Change to 2¾mm (size 2) needles.
Beg K row and patt row 17(21:11), work in st st from chart following markers for sleeves, inc one st each end of 5th, then every foll 5th(3rd:4th) row to 53(83:87) sts, then every foll 6th(4th:5th) row to 69(89:99) sts, working inc sts in patt.
Work straight until sleeve measures approx 19(23:28)cm [7½(9:11)in], ending patt row 18(2:12).

Shape top. Keeping patt correct, bind off 5 sts at beg off next 2 rows. Dec one st each end of every row to 49(57:63) sts, then every foll alt row to 37(47:57) sts, then every row to 27(33:33) sts. Bind off 4(5:5) sts at beg of next 4 rows. Bind off.

BUTTON BAND
With 2mm (size 0) needles and MC, cast on 11(11:15) sts.
Beg alt rows P1, work in K1, P1 rib until band, slightly stretched, fits up front to beg of neck shaping.
Leave sts on a holder. Sew band in place.
Mark positions on band for 5(5:6) buttons, the first approx 1.5cm (½in) from cast-on edge, last approx 4.5(5:5)cm [1¾(2:2)in] from holder and rem evenly spaced between.

BUTTONHOLE BAND
Work as given for button band, making buttonholes to match markers as follows:
BUTTONHOLE ROW 1 (right side) Rib 4(4:6), bind off 4, rib to end.
BUTTONHOLE ROW 2 Rib, casting on 4 sts over those bind off.

NECKBAND
Join shoulder seams.
With 2mm (size 0) needles, right side facing and MC, rib across front band sts, K right front neck sts, pick up 18(18:21) sts up right front neck, K back neck sts inc 4 sts, pick up 18(18:21) sts down left front neck, K left front neck sts, then rib across front band sts. 117(121:141) sts.
Work in rib as for front bands for 1.5cm (½in), making a buttonhole as before on rows 2 and 3.
With 2¾mm (size 2) needles, bind off in rib.

TO MAKE UP
Set in sleeves. Join side and sleeve seams. Sew on buttons.

Julian's Pullover
Shown on page 45, left

MEASUREMENTS
To fit approx age 6 mths (2 yrs:4 yrs).
Actual chest measurement 48(58.5:63.5)cm [19(23:25)in].
Length approx 30.5(37:40.5)cm [12(14½:16)in].
Sleeve seam approx 19(23:28)cm [7½(9:11)in].

MATERIALS
Rowan Lightweight DK 25g hanks; Main color (MC) Navy (97) 5(6:7) hanks, 1st contrasting color (A) Mid Blue (53) 1(1:2) hanks, 2nd contrasting color (B) Grey (60) 1(2:2) hanks, 3rd contrasting color (C) Light Blue (50) 1(1:2) hanks.
1 pair each of 2¾mm (size 2) and 3¼mm (size 3) knitting needles.

GAUGE
28 sts and 30 rows to 10cm (4in) square over patt on 3¼mm (size 3) needles.

Note When working patt from chart strand yarn not in use loosely across back of work over no more than 3 sts at a time, making sure that the same gauge is obtained throughout.

BACK
With 2¾mm (size 2) needles and MC, cast on 52(64:70) sts.
Work in K1, P1 rib for 4(5:5)cm [1½(2:2)in] inc to 67(81:87) sts in last row.
Change to 3¼mm (size 3) needles.

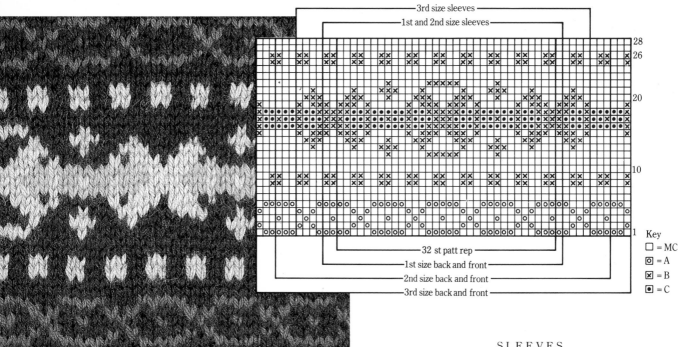

CHART AND KEY FOR JULIAN'S PULLOVER

•

Beg K row, work in st st from chart following markers for back until back measures approx 20.5(25.5:28)cm [8(10:11)in], ending patt row 20(4:12).

Shape armholes. Keeping patt correct, bind off 3(4:4) sts at beg of next 2 rows.
Dec one st each end of every row to 53(63:69) sts. Work straight until armholes measure 10(11.5:12.5)cm [4(4¹/₂:5)in], ending P row.

Shape shoulders. Bind off 6(8:9) sts at beg of next 4 rows. Leave rem sts on a holder.

FRONT
Work as given for back following markers for front until front measures 8(8:10) rows **less** than back to beg of shoulder shaping, ending P row.

Shape neck. NEXT ROW Patt 22(26:29), turn and leave rem sts on a spare needle.
Keeping patt correct, bind off 3 sts at neck edge on next and foll alt row. Dec one st at neck edge on every row to 12(16:18) sts.
Work 0(0:1) row straight, ending armhole edge.

Shape shoulder. Bind off 6(8:9) sts at beg of next row. Work 1 row. Bind off.
With right side facing sl center 9(11:11) sts on a holder, join yarn to rem sts and patt to end. Work 1 row. Complete to match first side.

SLEEVES
With 2³/₄mm (size 2) needles and MC, cast on 32(34:38) sts.
Work in K1, P1 rib for 4(5:5)cm [1¹/₂(2:2)in] inc to 35(35:43) sts in last row.
Change to 3¹/₄mm (size 3) needles.
Beg K row and patt row 5(7:1), work in st st from chart following markers for sleeves, inc one st each end of every 3rd row to 37(57:53) sts, then every foll 4th row to 49(63:71) sts, working inc sts in patt.
Work straight until sleeve measures approx 19(23:28)cm [7¹/₂(9:11)in], ending patt row 20(4:12).

Shape top. Keeping patt correct, bind off 3(4:4) sts at beg of next 2 rows. Dec one st each end of every row to 37(45:53) sts, then every foll alt row to 33(41:47) sts, then every row to 23(27:29) sts. Bind off 3(3:4) sts at beg of next 2 rows, then 3(4:4) sts at beg of foll 2 rows. Bind off.

TURTLENECK
Join right shoulder seam.
With 2³/₄mm (size 2) needles, right side facing and MC, pick up 16(16:18) sts down left front neck, K front neck sts inc 2 sts, pick up 16(16:18) sts up right front neck, then K back neck sts inc 4 sts. 76(80:86) sts.
Work in K1, P1 rib for 4(5:6.5)cm [1¹/₂(2:2¹/₂)in].
Change to 3¹/₄mm (size 3) needles and cont in rib until turtleneck measures 9.5(11.5:12.5)cm [3³/₄(4¹/₂:5)in]. Bind off loosely in rib.

TO MAKE UP
Join left shoulder and turtleneck seam reversing seam on turnback. Set in sleeves. Join side and sleeve seams.

JASMIN AND BABY ARABELLA LOOK PRETTY IN THEIR COLORFUL KNITS

·

Jasmin's Pullover

MEASUREMENTS
To fit approx age 6 mths (2 yrs:4 yrs).
Actual chest measurement 48(58.5:63.5)cm
[19(23:25)in].
Length approx 25.5(31.5:35.5)cm [10(12^{1}/$_{2}$:14)in].
Sleeve seam approx 19(23:28)cm [7^{1}/$_{2}$(9:11)in].

MATERIALS
Rowan 4ply Botany 25g hanks; Main color (MC) Red
(115) 5(6:7) hanks, 1st contrasting color (A) White (01)
1(2:2) hank, 2nd contrasting color (B) Green (124)
1(2:2) hank, 3rd contrasting color (C) Light Blue (51)
1(2:2) hank, 4th contrasting color (D) Yellow (12)
1(1:1) hank, 5th contrasting color (E) Dark Blue (108)
1(1:1) hank.
1 pair each of 2mm (size 0) and 2^{3}/$_{4}$mm (size 2) knitting

needles.
1 each of 2mm (size 0) and 2^{3}/$_{4}$mm (size 2) set of 4
double-pointed knitting needles.

GAUGE
40 sts and 44 rows to 10cm (4in) square over patt on
2^{3}/$_{4}$mm (size 2) needles.

Note When working patt from chart strand yarn not in
use loosely across back of work over no more than 3 sts
at a time, making sure that the same gauge is obtained
throughout.

BACK
With 2mm (size 0) needles and MC, cast on 76(94:102) sts.
Work in K1, P1 rib for 4(5:5)cm [1^{1}/$_{2}$(2:2)in] inc to
95(115:125) sts in last row.
Change to 2^{3}/$_{4}$mm (size 2) needles.

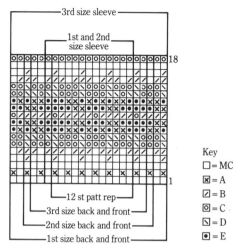

CHART AND COLOR KEY FOR JASMIN'S PULLOVER

Key
□ = MC
☒ = A
☑ = B
◉ = C
◨ = D
▣ = E

•

Beg K row, work in st st from chart following markers for back until back measures approx 15(20.5:23)cm [6(8:9)in], ending patt row 12(14:6).

Shape armholes. Keeping patt correct, bind off 5 sts at beg of next 2 rows. Dec one st each end of every row to 79(95:105) sts, then on every foll alt row to 75(89:99) sts.
Work straight until armholes measure 10(11.5:12.5)cm [4(4½:5)in], ending P row.

Shape shoulders. Bind off 9(11:13) sts at beg of next 2 rows, then 8(11:12) sts at beg of foll 2 rows.
Leave rem sts on a holder.

FRONT
Work as given for back following markers for front on chart until front measures 10(10:14) rows **less** than back to beg of shoulder shaping, ending P row.

Shape neck. NEXT ROW Patt 30(36:41), turn and leave rem sts on 4 spare needle.
Keeping patt correct, bind off 4 sts at neck edge on next row and 3(4:4) sts at beg of foll alt row. Dec one st at neck edge on every row to 17(22:25) sts. Work 0(0:2) rows straight, ending armhole edge.

Shape shoulders. Bind off 9(11:13) sts at beg of next row. Work 1 row. Bind off.
With right side facing sl center 15(17:17) sts on a holder, join yarn to rem sts and patt to end. Work 1 row. Complete to match first side.

SLEEVES
With 2mm (size 0) needles and MC, cast on 44(46:54) sts.
Work in K1, P1 rib for 4(5:5)cm [1½(2:2)in] inc to 49(49:59) sts in last row.

Change to 2¾mm (size 2) needles.
Beg K row and patt row 1(9:15), work in st st from chart following markers for sleeves, inc one st each end of 5th, then every foll 5th(3rd:4th) row to 53(83:87) sts, then on every foll 6th(4th:5th) row to 69(89:99) sts, working inc sts in patt.
Work straight until sleeve measures approx 19(23:28)cm [7½(9:11)in], ending patt row 12(14:6).

Shape top. Keeping patt correct, bind off 5 sts at beg of next 2 rows. Dec one st each end of every row to 49(57:63) sts, then every foll alt row to 37(47:57) sts, then every row to 27(33:33) sts. Bind off 4(5:5) sts at beg of next 4 rows. Bind off.

COLLAR
Join shoulder seams.
With 2mm (size 0) set of 4 needles, right side facing and MC, sl first 7(8:8) sts of center front neck onto another holder, K rem 8(9:9) sts inc one st, pick up 18(18:21) sts up right front neck, K back neck sts inc 3 sts, pick up 18(18:21) sts down left front neck inc one st, K rem front neck sts. 97(103:113) sts.
Work backwards and forwards in rows of rib as follows:
Beg alt rows P1, work in K1, P1 rib for 2.5cm (1in).
Change to 2¾mm (size 2) set of 4 needles and cont in rib until collar measures 4(4.5:5)cm [1½(1¾:2)in].
Bind off loosely in rib.

TO MAKE UP
Set in sleeves. Join side and sleeve seams. At center front catch-stitch first two sts together at base of collar to prevent neck from gaping.

•

Arabella's Vest

MEASUREMENTS
To fit approx age 6 mths (2 yrs:4 yrs).
Actual chest measurement 50(60.5:66)cm [19¾(23¾:26)in].
Length approx 25.5(31.5:35.5)cm [10(12½:14)in].

MATERIALS
Rowan 4ply Botany 25g hanks; Main color (MC) Cream (2) 3(4:5) hanks, 1st contrasting color (A) Red (115) 1(1:2) hanks, 2nd contrasting color (B) Navy (97) 1(1:2) hanks, 3rd contrasting color (C) Green (124) 1(1:1) hank, 4th contrasting color (D) Blue (56) 1(1:1) hank, 5th contrasting color (E) Yellow (629) 1(1:2) hanks.
1 pair each of 2mm (size 0) and 2¾mm (size 2) knitting needles.
5(6:6) small buttons.

GAUGE
40 sts and 44 rows to 10cm (4in) square over patt on 2¾mm (size 2) needles.

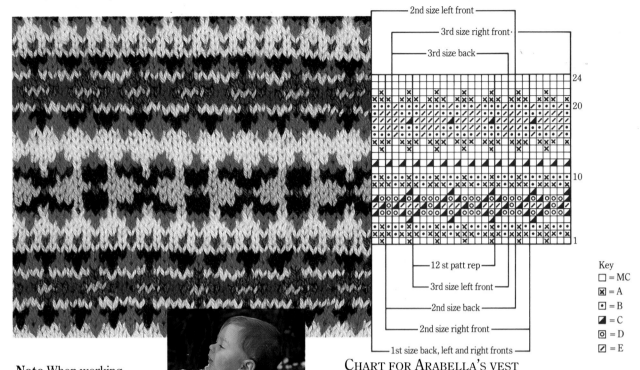

CHART FOR ARABELLA'S VEST

Key
□ = MC
⊠ = A
⊡ = B
◪ = C
⊚ = D
⊘ = E

Note When working patt from chart strand yarn not in use loosely across back of work over no more than 3 sts at a time, making sure the same gauge is obtained throughout.

BACK
With 2mm (size 0) needles and MC, cast on 76(94:102) sts.
Work in K1, P1 rib for 5(7.5:7.5)cm [2(3:3)in] inc to 95(115:125) sts in last row.
Change to 2³/₄mm (size 2) needles.
Beg K row, work in st st from chart following markers for back until back measures 15(20.5:23)cm [6(8:9)in], ending P row.

Shape armholes. Keeping patt correct, bind off 5 sts at beg of next 2 rows. Dec one st each end of every row to 79(95:105) sts, then on every foll alt row to 75(89:99) sts.
Work straight until armholes measure 10(11.5:12.5)cm [4(4¹/₂:5)in], ending P row.

Shape shoulders. Bind off 9(11:13) sts at beg of next 2 rows, then 8(11:12) sts at beg of foll 2 rows. Bind off.

LEFT FRONT
With 2mm (size 0) needles and MC, cast on 38(46:50) sts.
Work in K1, P1 rib for 5(7.5:7.5)cm [2(3:3)in] inc to 47(57:62) sts in last row.
Change to 2³/₄mm (size 2) needles.

Beg K row, work in st st from chart following markers for left front until front measures same as back to beg of armhole shaping, ending P row (for right front end K row here).

Shape armhole. Keeping patt correct, bind off 5 sts at beg of next row.
Work 1 row (omit this row when working right front).
Dec one st at armhole edge on every row to 39(47:52) sts, then on every foll alt row to 37(44:49) sts.
Work 1 row, ending P row.

Shape neck. NEXT ROW Keeping armhole edge straight, dec one st at neck edge on every row to 30(35:42) sts, then on every foll alt row to 17(22:25) sts (for right front work 1 row straight here), ending armhole edge.

Shape shoulder. Bind off 9(11:13) sts at beg of next row. Work 1 row. Bind off.

RIGHT FRONT
Work as given for left front, noting exceptions in parentheses and following markers for right front on chart.

BUTTON BAND
Join shoulder seams.
With 2mm (size 0) needles and MC, cast on 11(11:15) sts.
Beg alt rows P1, work in K1, P1 rib until band, slightly stretched, fits up front and across to center back neck. Bind off in rib. Sew band in place. Mark positions on band for 5(6:6) buttons, the first approx 1.5cm (¹/₂in)

from cast-on edge, the last at beg of neck shaping and rem evenly spaced between.

BUTTONHOLE BAND
Work as given for button band, making buttonholes to match markers as follows:
BUTTONHOLE ROW 1 (right side) Rib 4(4:6), bind off 4, rib to end.
BUTTONHOLE ROW 2 Rib, binding on 4 sts over those bound off.

ARMHOLE BANDS
With 2mm (size 0) needles, right side facing and MC, pick up 90(96:102) sts around armhole edge.
Work in K1, P1 rib for 1.5cm (¹⁄₂in), dec one st each end of every row. Bind off in rib.

TO MAKE UP
Join side and armhole band seams. Join bound-off edges of front bands together at center back neck. Sew on buttons.

•

Laura's Pullover and Cardigan

MEASUREMENTS
To fit approx age 6 mths (2 yrs:4 yrs).
Actual chest measurement: cardigan 51(61.5:67.5)cm [20(24¹⁄₄:26¹⁄₂)in], pullover 47(58:63)cm [18¹⁄₂(22³⁄₄:24³⁄₄)in].
Length: cardigan 25.5(31.5:35.5)cm [10(12¹⁄₂:14)in], pullover 25(31:35)cm [9³⁄₄(12¹⁄₄:13³⁄₄)in].
Sleeve seam (both garments) 19(23:28)cm [7¹⁄₂(9:11)in].

MATERIALS
Rowan 4ply Botany 25g hanks (for both garments); Main color (MC) Red (115) 8(10:12) hanks, 1st contrasting color (A) Yellow (629) 2(2:2) hanks, 2nd contrasting color (B) Green (405) 2(2:2) hanks, 3rd contrasting color (C) White (01) 2(2:2) hanks.
1 pair each of 2mm (size 0) and 2³⁄₄mm (size 2) knitting needles.
Cardigan 5(6:6) small buttons. Pullover 3 small buttons. crochet hook.

GAUGE
34 sts and 46 rows to 10cm (4in) square over st st on 2³⁄₄mm (size 2) needles.
40 sts and 44 rows to 10cm (4in) square over patt on 2³⁄₄mm (size 2) needles.

Note When working patt from chart strand yarn not in use loosely across back of work over no more than 3 sts at a time, making sure that the same gauge is obtained throughout.

CARDIGAN

BACK
With 2mm (size 0) needles and MC, cast on 76(94:102) sts.
Work in K1, P1 rib for 4(5:5)cm [1¹⁄₂(2:2)in] inc to 83(101:109) sts in last row.
Change to 2³⁄₄mm (size 2) needles.
Beg K row, work in st st until back measures 15(20.5:23)cm [6(8:9)in], ending P row.

Shape armholes. Bind off 3(5:5) sts at beg of next 2 rows. Dec one st each end of every row to 71(81:93) sts, then every foll alt row to 69(79:89) sts.
Work 3(5:9) rows straight, ending P row.
Beg K row, work in st st from chart (page 54) following markers for cardigan back until 34 rows of chart have been worked.
Now cont in MC only. Work 2 rows, ending P row.

Shape shoulders. Bind off 8(10:12) sts at beg of next 4 rows. Bind off rem sts.

LEFT FRONT
With 2mm (size 0) needles and MC, cast on 38(46:50) sts.
Work in K1, P1 rib for 4(5:5)cm [1¹⁄₂(2:2)in] inc to 41(50:54) sts in last row.
Change to 2³⁄₄mm (size 2) needles.
Beg K row, work in st st until front measures same as back to beg of armhole shaping, ending P row (for right front end K row here).

Shape armhole. Bind off 3(5:5) sts at beg of next row.
Work 1 row (omit this row when working right front).
Dec one st at armhole edge on every row to 35(40:46) sts, then on every foll alt row to 34(39:44) sts.

Shape neck. Dec one st at neck edge on next and foll 1(2:4) alt rows, ending P row. 32(36:39) sts.
Beg K row, work in st st from chart, following markers for cardigan left front, AT THE SAME TIME, dec one st at front edge on foll alt rows from last dec to 19(23:29) sts, then on every foll 3rd row to 16(20:24) sts, work in MC when the 34 rows of chart have been worked.
Work 1 row straight (for right front work 2 rows straight here), ending armhole edge.

Shape shoulder. Bind off 8(10:12) sts at beg of next row. Work 1 row. Bind off.

RIGHT FRONT
Work as given for left front, noting exceptions in parentheses and following markers for cardigan right front on chart.

•

LAURA'S FAIR ISLE CARDIGAN AND PULLOVER

SLEEVES

With 2mm (size 0) needles and MC, bind on 42(46:54) sts.
Work in K1, P1 rib for 4(5:5)cm [1½(2:2)in].
Change to 2¾mm (size 2) needles.
Beg K row, work in st st, inc one st each end of 5th, then every foll 5th(4th:5th) row to 46(70:72) sts, then on every foll 6th(5th:6th) row to 62(78:88) sts.
Work straight until sleeve measures 19(23:28)cm [7½(9:11)in], ending P row.

Shape top. Bind off 3(5:5) sts at beg of next 2 rows.
Dec one st each end of every row to 50(58:64) sts, then every foll alt row to 32(40:48) sts, then every row to 24 sts. Bind off 3 sts at beg of next 4 rows. Bind off.

BUTTON BAND

Join shoulder seams.
With 2mm (size 0) needles and MC, cast on 11(11:15) sts.
Beg alt rows P1, work in K1, P1 rib until band, slightly stretched, fits up front and across to center back neck. Bind off in rib. Sew band in place.
Mark positions on band for 5(6:6) buttons, the first approx 1.5cm (½in) from cast-on edge, the last at beg of neck shaping and rem evenly spaced between.

BUTTONHOLE BAND

Work as given for button band, making buttonholes to match markers as follows:

BUTTONHOLE ROW 1 (right side) Rib 4(4:6), bind off 4, rib to end.
BUTTONHOLE ROW 2 Rib, binding on 4 sts over those bound off.

TO MAKE UP

Set in sleeves. Join side and sleeve seams. Join bands together at center back neck. Sew on buttons.

PULLOVER

BACK

With 2mm (size 0) needles and MC, cast on 72(90:98) sts.
Work in K1, P1 rib for 4(5:5)cm [1½(2:2)in] inc to 79(97:105) sts in last row.
Change to 2¾mm (size 2) needles.
Beg K row, work in st st until back measures 14.5(19.5:22)cm [5¾(7¾:8¾)in], ending P row.

Shape armholes. Bind off 3(5:5) sts at beg of next 2 rows. Dec one st each end of every row to 67(77:89) sts, then every foll alt row to 65(75:85) sts.
Work 3(5:9) rows straight, ending P row.
Beg K row, work in st st from chart, following markers for pullover back until 34 rows of chart have been worked.
Now cont in MC only. Work 2 rows, ending P row.

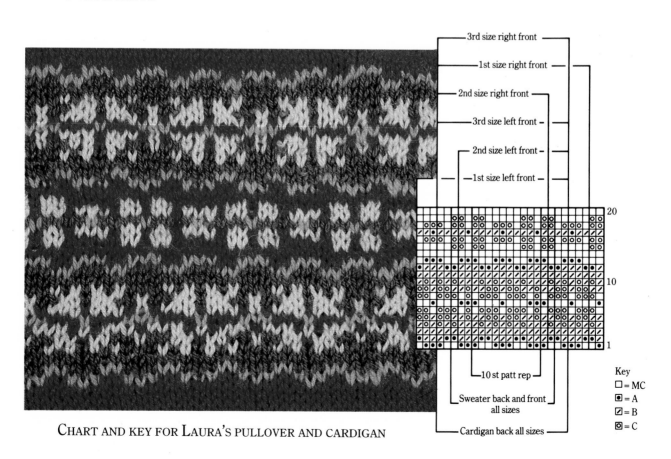

CHART AND KEY FOR LAURA'S PULLOVER AND CARDIGAN

Shape shoulders. Bind off 7(9:11) sts at beg of next 4 rows. Leave rem sts on a holder.

FRONT

Work as given for back following markers for pullover front on chart until front measures 10(10:14) rows **less** than back to beg of shoulder shaping, ending P row.

Shape neck. NEXT ROW Patt 26(30:35), turn and leave rem sts on a spare needle.
Keeping patt correct as back, bind off 3 sts at beg of next and foll alt row. Dec one st at neck edge on every row to 14(18:22) sts.
Work 0(0:3) rows straight, ending armhole edge.

Shape shoulder. Bind off 7(9:11) sts at beg of next row. Work 1 row. Bind off.
With right side facing sl center 13(15:15) sts on a holder, join yarn to rem sts and patt to end.
Work 1 row. Complete to match first side.

SLEEVES

With 2mm (size 0) needles and MC, cast on 38(42:50) sts.
Work in K1, P1 rib for 4(5:5)cm [1^1/$_2$(2:2)in].
Change to 2^3/$_4$mm (size 2) needles.
Beg K row, work in st st, inc one st each end of 5th and every foll 5th(4th:5th) row to 42(66:68) sts, then on every foll 6th(5th:6th) row to 58(74:84) sts.
Work straight until sleeve measures 19(23:28)cm [7^1/$_2$(9:11)in], ending P row.

Shape top. Bind off 3(5:5) sts at beg of next 2 rows. Dec one st each end of every row to 46(50:56) sts, then on every foll alt row to 30(34:38) sts, then every row to 24 sts. Bind off 3 sts at beg of next 4 rows. Bind off.

NECKBAND

Join right shoulder seam.
With 2mm (size 0) needles, right side facing and MC, pick up 18(18:21) sts down left front neck, K front neck sts inc 3 sts, pick up 18(18:21) sts up right front neck, then K back neck sts inc 5 sts. 94(98:106) sts.
Work in K1, P1 rib for 1.5cm (^{1}/$_2$in). With 2^3/$_4$mm (size 2) needles, bind off in rib.

TO MAKE UP

Crochet a row of slip stitch across left back shoulder and neckband. Crochet a row of slip stitch across left front shoulder and neckband, then work another row on this edge, working 3 button loops evenly spaced. Overlap front crochet border over back and catch together at armhole edge. Set in sleeves. Join side and sleeve seams. Sew buttons on back border to match loops on front border.

Chelsea's Pullover

MEASUREMENTS

To fit approx age 6 mths (2 yrs:4 yrs).
Actual chest measurement 48(58.5:63.5)cm [19(23:25)in].
Length 25.5(31.5:35.5)cm [10(12^1/$_2$:14)in].
Sleeve seam 19(23:28)cm [7^1/$_2$(9:11)in].

MATERIALS

Rowan Lightweight DK 25g hanks; Main color (MC) Mid-Beige (82) 6(7:8) hanks, 1st contrasting color (A) Rose Pink (412) 1(1:1) hank, 2nd contrasting color (B) Brown (98) 1(1:1) hank, 3rd contrasting color (C) Cream (02) 1(1:1) hank, 4th contrasting color (D) Light Beige (614) 1(1:1) hank.
1 pair each of 2^3/$_4$mm (size 2) and 3^1/$_4$mm (size 3) knitting needles.
1 each of 2^3/$_4$mm (size 2), 3mm (size 2) and 3^1/$_4$mm (size 3) set of 4 double-pointed knitting needles.

GAUGE

26 sts and 34 rows to 10cm (4in) square over st st on 3^1/$_4$mm (size 3) needles.
28 sts and 30 rows to 10cm (4in) square over patt on 3^1/$_4$mm (size 3) needles.

Note When working in Fair Isle patt strand yarn not in use loosely across back of work over no more than 3 sts at a time, making sure that the same gauge is obtained throughout.

BACK AND FRONT (alike)

With 2^3/$_4$mm (size 2) needles and MC, cast on 54(68:74) sts.

Work in K1, P1 rib for 4(5:5)cm [1½(2:2)in] inc to 62(76:82) sts in last row.
Change to 3¼mm (size 3) needles.
Beg K row, work in st st until work measures 15(20.5:23)cm [6(8:9)in], ending P row.

Shape armholes. Bind off 2(3:3) sts at beg of next 2 rows. Dec one st each end of every row to 52(62:68) sts. Work 9(8:8) rows straight, ending P row.

Divide for yoke. K18(22:24), turn and leave rem sts on a spare needle.
NEXT ROW P1, P2 tog, P to end.
NEXT ROW K to last 3 sts, K2 tog, K1.
Rep last 2 rows to 6(6:8) sts.
NEXT ROW P.
NEXT ROW K to last 3 sts, K2 tog, K1.
Rep last 2 rows to 3 sts.
NEXT ROW P.
NEXT ROW K2 tog, K1.
NEXT ROW P.
K2 tog and fasten off.
With right side facing, sl center 16(18:20) sts on a holder, join yarn to rem sts, K to end.
NEXT ROW P to last 3 sts, P2 tog tbl, P1.
NEXT ROW K1, sl 1, K1, psso, K to end.
Rep last 2 rows to 6(6:8) sts.
NEXT ROW P.
NEXT ROW K1, sl 1, K1, psso, K to end.
Rep last 2 rows to 3 sts.
NEXT ROW P.
NEXT ROW P.
NEXT ROW K1, sl 1, K1, psso.
K2 tog and fasten off.

YOKE

With 3¼mm (size 3) set of 4 needles, right side facing and MC, pick up 22(26:30) sts down left front neck, K front neck sts inc 4(6:4) sts, pick up 22(26:30) sts up right front neck, 22(26:30) sts down right back neck, K back neck sts inc 4(6:4) sts, then pick up 22(26:30) sts up left back neck. 128(152:168) sts.
Place a marker at beg of round and work in **rounds** (K every round) as follows:
Work 0(1:2) rounds in MC.
NEXT ROUND [1A, 1B] to end.
Work 1(2:2) rounds in A.
NEXT ROUND [3A, 1C] to end.
NEXT ROUND [1D, 1A, 3D, 1A, 2D] to end.
NEXT ROUND [3B, 1C, 2B, with C K2 tog] to end. 112(133:147) sts.
NEXT ROUND [2A, 3B, 1A, 1B] to end.
NEXT ROUND [3D, 1C, 2D, 1C] to end.
NEXT ROUND [2A, 3B, 1A, 1B] to end.
NEXT ROUND [3B, 1C, 2B, 1C] to end.
Change to 2¾mm (size 2) set of 4 needles.

•

LAURA AND CHELSEA IN THEIR SMART FAIR ISLES

DETAIL OF THE PATTERN ON LAURA'S AND CHELSEA'S KNITS

•

NEXT ROUND [1D, 1A, 3D, 1A, 1D] to end.
NEXT ROUND [3A, 1C, 2A, 1C] to end.
Work 1(2:2) rounds in A, 1 round in C.
NEXT ROUND With MC, [K5, K2 tog] to end.
96(114:126) sts.
Work 1 round in C and 0(1:2) rounds in MC, dec to
80(88:94) sts evenly in last round.
Change to $2^{3}/_{4}$mm (size 2) set of 4 needles.
Work in MC only in rounds of K1, P1 rib for 3cm
[$1^{1}/_{4}$in].
With $3^{1}/_{4}$mm (size 3) set of 4 needles, bind off loosely in
rib.

SLEEVES

With $2^{3}/_{4}$mm (size 2) needles and MC, cast on 32(34:40)
sts.
Work in K1, P1 rib for 4(5:5)cm [$1^{1}/_{2}$(2:2)in].
Change to $3^{1}/_{4}$mm (size 3) needles.
Beg K row, work in st st, inc one st each end of 3rd and
every foll 5th(4th:5th) row to 46(58:66) sts.
Work straight until sleeve measures 19(23:28)cm
[$7^{1}/_{2}$(9:11)in], ending P row.

Shape top. Bind off 2(3:3) sts at beg of next 2 rows.
Dec one st each end of every row to 36(46:54) sts, then
every foll alt row to 30(38:46) sts, then on every row to
16(20:20) sts. Bind off 2(3:3) sts at beg of next 2 rows,
then 3 sts at beg of foll 2 rows. Bind off.

TO MAKE UP

Fold neckband in half to inside and sew in place. Set in
sleeves. Join side and sleeve seams.

Laura's Pullover

MEASUREMENTS

To fit approx age 6 mths (2 yrs:4 yrs).
Actual chest measurement 48)58.5:63.5)cm
[19(23:25)in].
Length 25.5(31.5:35.5)cm [10(12$^{1}/_{2}$:14)in].
Sleeve seam 19(23:28)cm [7$^{1}/_{2}$(9:11)in].

MATERIALS

Rowan Lightweight DK 25g hanks; Main color (MC)
Green (606) 6(7:8) hanks, 1st contrasting color (A)
Rose Pink (412) 1(1:1) hank, 2nd contrasting color (B)
Lilac (92) 1(1:1) hank, 3rd contrasting color (C) Pale
Green (605) 1(1:1) hank, 4th contrasting color (D)
Light Blue (108) 1(1:1) hank.
1 pair each of $2^{3}/_{4}$mm (size 2) and $3^{1}/_{4}$ (size 3) knitting
needles. 1 each of $2^{3}/_{4}$mm (size 2), and $3^{1}/_{4}$mm (size 3)
set of 4 double-pointed knitting
needles.

GAUGE

26 sts and 34 rows to 10cm (4in) square over st st on
$3^{1}/_{4}$mm (size 3) needles.
28 sts and 30 rows to 10cm (4in) square over patt on
$3^{1}/_{4}$mm (size 3) needles.

Note When working in Fair Isle patt strand yarn not in
use loosely across back of work over no more than 3 sts
at a time, making sure that the same gauge is obtained
throughout.

LAURA IN HER GREEN FAIR ISLE PULLOVER

•

BACK, FRONT, YOKE, SLEEVES AND
TO MAKE UP
Work as given for back, front, yoke, sleeves and to
make up as Chelsea's pullover, but work neck rib on
2³/₄mm (size 2) set of 4 needles for 4(5:6.5)cm
[1¹/₂(2:2¹/₂)in]. Change to 3¹/₄mm (size 3) set of 4
needles and cont in rib until turtleneck measures
9.5(11.5:12.5)cm [3³/₄(4¹/₂:5)in]. Fold turtleneck to
right side; do not sew in place.

Edward's Pullover

Shown on page 60

MEASUREMENTS
To fit approx age 6 mths (2 yrs:4 yrs).
Actual chest measurement 48(58.5:63.5)cm
[19(23:25)in].
Length approx 30.5(37:40.5)cm [12(14¹/₂:16)in].
Sleeve seam approx 19(23:28)cm [7¹/₂(9:11)in].

MATERIALS
Rowan 4ply Botany 25g hanks; Main color (MC) Beige
(82) 5(6:7) hanks; 1st contrasting color (A) Blue (56)
1(1:2) hanks, 2nd contrasting color (B) Green (124)
1(1:2) hanks, 3rd contrasting color (C) Orange (26)
1(1:2) hanks, 4th contrasting color (D) Light Blue (51)
1(1:1) hank, 5th contrasting color (E) Yellow (629)
1(1:2) hanks, 6th contrasting color (F) Light Beige
(614) 1(1:1) hank. 1 pair each of 2mm (size 0) and 2³/₄
(size 2) knitting needles.

GAUGE
40 sts and 44 rows to 10cm (4in) square over patt on
2³/₄mm (size 2) needles.

Note When working patt from chart strand yarn not in
use loosely across back of work over no more than 3 sts
at a time, making sure that the same gauge is obtained
throughout.

BACK
* With 2mm (size 0) needles and MC, cast on
76(94:102) sts.
Work in K1, P1 rib for 4(5:5)cm [1¹/₂(2:2)in] inc to
95(115:125) sts in last row.
Change to 2³/₄mm (size 2) needles.
Beg K row, work in st st from chart following markers
for back until back measures approx 20.5(25.5:28)cm
[8(10:11)in], ending patt row 30(4:14).

Shape armholes. Keeping patt correct, bind off 5 sts
at beg of next 2 rows.
Dec one st each end of every row to 79(95:105) sts,
then on every foll alt row to 75(89:99) sts *.
Work straight until armholes measure approx
10(11.5:12.5)cm [4(4¹/₂:5)in], ending patt row
32(10:28).

Shape shoulders. Bind off 9(11:13) sts at beg of next
2 rows, then 8(11:12) sts at beg of foll 2 rows.
Leave rem sts on a holder.

FRONT
Work as given for back from * to *.
Work 1 row, ending P row.

Shape neck. NEXT ROW Patt 37(44:49), turn and leave
rem sts on a spare needle.
Keeping patt correct and armhole edge straight, dec
one st at neck edge on every row to 30(35:42) sts, then
every foll alt row to 17(22:25) sts (for right side of front
work 1 row straight here), ending armhole edge.

Shape shoulder. Bind off 9(11:13) sts at beg of next
row. Work 1 row. Bind off.
With right side facing sl center st on a safety pin, join
yarn to rem sts and patt to end. Complete to match first
side, noting exception in parentheses.

SLEEVES
With 2mm (size 0) needles and MC, cast on 44(46:54)
sts.
Work in K1, P1 rib for 4(5:5)cm [1¹/₂(2:2)in] inc to
49(49:59) sts in last row.
Change to 2³/₄mm (size 2) needles.
Beg K row and patt row 7(11:1), work in st st from
chart following markers for sleeves, inc one st each end
of 5th, then every foll 5th(3rd:4th) row to 53(83:87)
sts, then on every foll 6th(4th:5th) row to 69(89:99)
sts, working inc sts in patt.
Work straight until sleeve measures approx

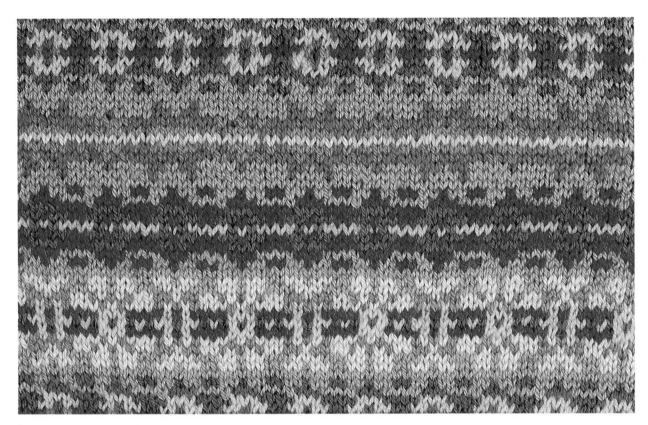

19(23:28)cm [7¹/₂(9:11)in], ending patt row 30(4:14).

Shape top. Keeping patt correct, bind off 5 sts at beg of next 2 rows. Dec one st each end of every row to 49(57:63) sts, then every foll alt row to 37(47:57) sts, then every row to 27(33:33) sts. Bind off 4(5:5) sts at beg of next 4 rows. Bind off.

NECKBAND

Join right shoulder seam. With 2mm (size 0) needles, right side facing and MC, pick up 36(38:44) sts down left front neck, K center front st, pick up 36(38:44) sts up right front neck, K back neck sts. 114(120:138) sts. Work 1 row in K1, P1 rib. Cont in rib and dec one st each side of center front st on every row for 1.5cm (¹/₂in). Bind off in rib, dec as before.

TO MAKE UP

Join left shoulder and neckband seam. Set in sleeves. Join side and sleeve seams.

•

EDWARD'S PULLOVER

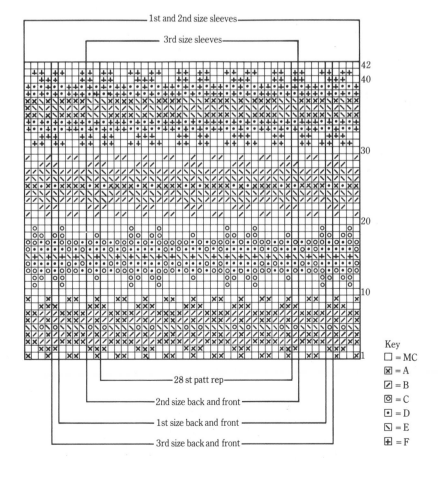

Key
□ = MC
⊠ = A
⊿ = B
⊙ = C
• = D
⊠ = E
⊞ = F

SCANDINAVIAN

HAVING GROWN UP in Sweden, I have worn Scandinavian-style pullovers since my childhood, so they are naturally my favorites. The traditional Scandinavian designs have continued almost unchanged over many, many years, and are as popular today as they ever were. Perfect for skiing or skating, or for any winter activities, they are warm and practical as well as lovely to look at.

Oliver's Turtleneck

MEASUREMENTS
To fit approx age 6 mths (2 yrs:4 yrs).
Actual chest measurement 48(58.5:63.5)cm
[19(23:25)in].
Length 30.5(37:40.5)cm [12(14¹/₂:16)in].
Sleeve seam 19(23:28)cm [7¹/₂(9:11)in].

MATERIALS
Rowan Lightweight DK 25g hanks; Main color (MC)
Navy (97) 7(8:9) hanks, 1st contrasting color (A)
Cream (02) 2(2:2) hanks, 2nd contrasting color (B) Red
(115) 1(1:1) hank, 3rd contrasting color (C) Grey (60)
1(1:1) hank, 4th contrasting color (D) Dark Blue (55)
1(1:1) hank, 5th contrasting color (E) Light Blue (50)
1(1:1) hank.
1 pair each of 2³/₄mm (size 2) and 3¹/₄mm (size 3)
knitting needles.

GAUGE
28 sts and 30 rows to 10cm (4in) square over patt on
3¹/₄mm (size 3) needles.

Note When working patt from chart strand yarn not in
use loosely across back of work over no more than 3 sts
at a time, making sure that the same gauge is obtained
throughout. When working first line of snowflakes, and
when repeating this line, omit the snowflakes at beg
and end of rows. Work second line of snowflakes as
shown.

BACK
With 2³/₄mm (size 2) needles and MC, cast on 52(64:70)
sts.
Work in K1, P1 rib for 4(5:5)cm [1¹/₂(2:2)in] inc to
67(81:87) sts in last row.
Change to 3¹/₄mm (size 3) needles.
Beg K row, work in st st from chart 1 following
markers for back, work rows 1 to 6, then rep rows 7 to
24 2(3:3) times, then work row 7(0:7) to row 8(0:14),
ending patt row 8(24:14).
Now work rows 25 to 54, then row 25 to row
28(28:30), ending P row.

Shape shoulders. Keeping patt correct, bind off
9(12:13) sts at beg of next 2 rows, then 8(11:12) sts at
beg of foll 2 rows. Leave rem sts on a holder.

FRONT
Work as back, following markers for front, until front is
8(8:10) rows **less** than back to beg of shoulder shaping,
ending P row.

Shape neck. NEXT ROW Patt 28(34:37), turn and leave
rem sts on a spare needle.
Keeping patt correct, bind off 4 sts at neck edge on
next row and 3 sts on foll alt row. Dec one st at neck
edge on every row to 17(23:25) sts.
Work 0(0:1) row straight, ending side edge.

Shape shoulder. Bind off 9(12:13) sts at beg of next
row. Work 1 row. Bind off.
With right side facing sl center 11(13:13) sts on a
holder, join yarn to rem sts and patt to end. Work 1
row. Complete to match first side.

SLEEVES
With 2³/₄mm (size 2) needles and MC, cast on 32(32:40)
sts.
Work in K1, P1 rib for 4(5:5)cm [1¹/₂(2:2)in] inc to
33(33:41) sts in last row.
Change to 3¹/₄mm (size 3) needles.
Beg K row, work in st st from chart 1 following
markers for sleeves, work rows 1 to 6, then rep rows 7
to 24 1(2:3) times, then work row 7(7:0) to row
18(8:0), then rows 1 to 6 again, AT THE SAME TIME,
inc one st each end of 3rd, then every foll 4th(3rd:4th)
row to 53(63:57) sts, then on **3rd size only** inc one st
each end of every 5th row to 69 sts, working straight
after last inc and work inc sts in patt on **all sizes**, but
do not work snowflakes too near to row ends.
Work 2 rows in MC. Bind off.

TURTLENECK
Join right shoulder seam.
With 2³/₄mm (size 2) needles, right side facing and MC,
pick up 16(16:18) sts down left front neck, K front neck
sts inc 2 sts, pick up 16(16:18) sts up right front neck,

K back neck sts inc 4 sts. 82(86:92) sts.
Work in K1, P1 rib for 4(5:6.5)cm [1¹/₂(2:2¹/₂)in].
Change to 3¹/₄mm (size 3) needles and cont in rib until
turtleneck measures 9.5(11.5:12.5)cm [3³/₄(4¹/₂:5)in].
Bind off loosely in rib.

TO MAKE UP
Join left shoulder and turtleneck seam, reversing seam
on turnback. Sew on sleeves placing center of bound-off
edges at shoulder seams. Join side and sleeve seams.

Antonia's Cardigan
Shown on page 62

MEASUREMENTS
To fit approx age 6 mths (2 yrs:4 yrs).
Actual chest measurement 51(61.5:65.5)cm
[20(24¹/₄:25³/₄)in].
Length 30.5(37:40.5)cm [12(14¹/₂:16)in].
Sleeve seam 19(23:28)cm [7¹/₂(9:11)in].

MATERIALS
Rowan Lightweight DK 25g hanks; Main color (MC)
Red (115) 7(8:9) hanks; 1st contrasting color (A) White
(01) 2(2:2) hanks, 2nd contrasting color (B) Black (62)

1(1:1) hank, 3rd contrasting color (C) Dark Grey (61)
1(1:1) hank, 4th contrasting color (D) Light Grey (60)
1(1:1) hank, 5th contrasting color (E) Dark Blue (55)
1(1:1) hank.
1 pair each of 2³/₄mm (size 2) and 3¹/₄mm (size 3)
knitting needles.
7(8:9) small buttons.

GAUGE
28 sts and 30 rows to 10cm (4in) square over patt on
3¹/₄mm (size 3) needles.

Note When working patt from chart strand yarn not in
use loosely across back of work over no more than 3 sts
at a time, making sure that the same gauge is obtained
throughout. When working first line of snowflakes, and
when repeating this line, omit the snowflakes at beg
and end of rows. Work second line of snowflakes as
shown.

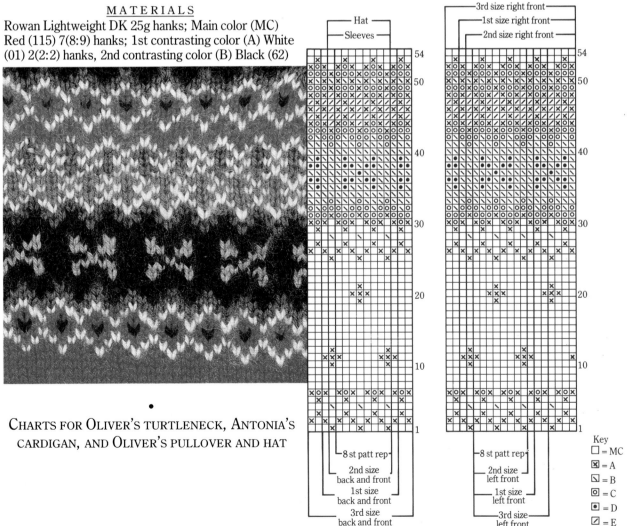

CHARTS FOR OLIVER'S TURTLENECK, ANTONIA'S
CARDIGAN, AND OLIVER'S PULLOVER AND HAT

BACK

Work as given for back of Oliver's turtleneck pullover (page 64).

LEFT FRONT

With 2³/₄mm (size 2) needles and MC, cast on 26(32:36) sts.
Work in K1, P1 rib for 4(5:5)cm [1¹/₂(2:2)in] inc to 33(40:43) sts in last row.
Change to 3¹/₄mm (size 3) needles.
Work in patt row sequence as back, but working from chart 2, following markers for left front until front is 8(8:10) rows (for right front read 7[7:9] rows here) **less** than back to shoulders, ending side edge.

Shape neck. NEXT ROW Patt 28(34:37), turn and leave rem sts on a holder.
Keeping patt correct, bind off 4 sts at neck edge on next row and 3 sts on foll alt row. Dec one st at neck edge on every row to 17(23:25) sts.
Work 0(0:1) row straight, ending side edge.

Shape shoulder. Bind off 9(12:13) sts at beg of next row. Work 1 row. Bind off.

RIGHT FRONT

Work as given for left front following markers on chart 2 for right front and noting exception in parentheses.

SLEEVES

Work as given for sleeves of Oliver's turtleneck sweater (page 64).

BUTTON BAND

With 2³/₄mm (size 2) needles and MC, cast on 11 sts.
Beg alt rows P1, work in K1, P1 rib until band, slightly stretched, fits up front to beg of neck shaping. Bind off in rib. Sew in place.
Mark positions on band for 7(8:9) buttons, the first and last approx 1.5cm (¹/₂in) from cast-on and bound-off edges and rem evenly spaced between.

BUTTONHOLE BAND

Work as given for button band making buttonholes to match markers as follows:
BUTTONHOLE ROW 1 (right side) Rib 5, bind off 2, rib to end.
BUTTONHOLE ROW 2 Rib binding 2 sts over those bound off.

COLLAR

Join shoulder seams.
With 2³/₄mm (size 2) needles, right side facing and MC, K right front neck sts inc one st, pick up 16(16:18) sts up right front neck, K back neck sts inc 4 sts, pick up 16(16:18) sts down left front neck, K left front neck sts inc one st. 81(85:91) sts.
Beg alt rows P1, work in K1, P1 rib for 2.5cm (1in).
Change to 3¹/₄mm (size 3) needles and cont in rib until collar measures 5(5.5:6.5)cm [2(2¹/₄:2¹/₂)in].
Bind off in rib.

TO MAKE UP

Sew on sleeves placing center of bound-off edges at shoulder seams. Join side and sleeve seams. Sew on buttons.

•

Oliver's Pullover

MEASUREMENTS

To fit approx age 6 mths (2 yrs:4 yrs).
Actual chest measurement 48(58.5:63.5)cm [19(23:25)in].
Length 30.5(37:40.5)cm [12(14¹/₂:16)in].
Sleeve seam 19(23:28)cm [7¹/₂(9:11)in].

MATERIALS

Rowan Lightweight DK 25g hanks; Main color (MC) Black (62) 7(8:9) hanks, 1st contrasting color (A) Cream (02) 2(2:2) hanks, 2nd contrasting color (B) Mustard (08) 1(1:1) hank, 3rd contrasting color (C) Dark Grey (61) 1(1:1) hank, 4th contrasting color (D) Green (606) 1(1:1) hank, 5th contrasting color (E) Light Grey (60) 1(1:1) hank.
1 pair each of 2³/₄mm (size 2) and 3¹/₄mm (size 3) knitting needles.
crochet hook.
2 buttons.

GAUGE

28 sts and 30 rows to 10cm (4in) square over patt on 3¹/₄mm (size 3) needles.

Note When working patt from chart strand yarn when not in use loosely across back of work over no more than 3 sts at a time, making sure that the same gauge is obtained throughout. When working first line of snowflakes, and when repeating this line, omit the snowflakes at beg and end of rows. Work second line of snowflakes as shown.

BACK, FRONT AND SLEEVES

Work as given for back, front and sleeves of Oliver's turtleneck sweater (page 64).

NECKBAND

Work as given for turtleneck of Oliver's turtleneck sweater, but working in rib for only 1.5cm (¹/₂in).

TO MAKE UP

Join left shoulder seam for 3(5:5.5)cm [1¹/₄(2:2¹/₄)in] leaving remainder of shoulder and neckband open. Crochet a row of slip stitch around shoulder opening, then another row of slip stitch along front edge only, working 2 button loops. Sew buttons on back edge to match. Complete as Oliver's turtleneck sweater.

TOP OLIVER'S HAT WITH A THICK POMPOM. INSTRUCTIONS ARE ON PAGE 111

•

Scandinavian Hat

MEASUREMENTS
To suit approx age 2 yrs (4 yrs)

MATERIALS
Rowan Lightweight DK 25g hanks; Main color (MC) Black (62) 1(1) hank, 1st contrasting color (A) Cream (02) 1(1) hank, 2nd contrasting color (B) Mustard (08) 1(1) hank, 3rd contrasting color (C) Dark Grey (61) 1(1) hank, 4th contrasting color (D) Green (606) 1(1) hank, 5th contrasting color (E) Light Grey (60) 1(1) hank.
1 pair each of 2³/₄mm (size 2) and 3¹/₄mm (size 3) knitting needles.

GAUGE
28 sts and 30 rows to 10cm (4in) square over patt on 3¹/₄mm (size 3) needles.

Note When working patt from chart strand yarn not in use loosely across back of work over no more than 3 sts at a time, making sure that the same gauge is obtained throughout.

With 3¹/₄mm (size 3) needles and MC, cast on 104(120) sts.

Change to 2³/₄mm (size 2) needles and work in K2, P2 rib for 1.5(2)cm [¹/₂(³/₄)in] inc to 129(145) sts in last row. Change to 3¹/₄m (size 3) needles.
Beg K row, work in st st from chart 1 (page 65), following markers for hat, work row 29(25) to row 53, ending wrong side row.
DEC ROW With MC, P3(6), * P2 tog, P9(10); rep from * to last 5(7) sts, P2 tog, P3(5). 117(133) sts.
With MC, work 2 rows.
DEC ROW With MC, K7(6), * K2 tog, K15(13); rep from * to last 8(7) sts, K2 tog, K6(5). 110(124) sts.
NEXT ROW P0(4)MC, * 1A, 4MC; rep from * to end.
NEXT ROW With MC, K4(6), * K2 tog, K3; rep from * to last 6(3) sts, K2 tog, K4(1). 89(100) sts.
NEXT ROW With MC, P.
NEXT ROW K0(2)MC, * 1A, 3MC; rep from * to last 1(2) sts, 1A, 0(1)MC.
NEXT ROW With MC, P1(0), [P2 tog] to end. 45(50) sts.
With MC, K 1 row and P 1 row dec 4(1) sts in first row. 41(49) sts.
Now work row 1 to row 4(6) from chart 1.
With MC, K 1 row.
NEXT ROW With MC, [P2 tog] to last st, P1. 21(25) sts.
Break off yarn, leaving a long end. Run end through rem sts, draw up tightly, secure, then join back seam. Make a pompom using all colors, and attach to top of hat.

TYROLEAN EMBROIDERED

FLOWERS ARE typical of the Tyrolean style. Here a very simple flower motif is embroidered on the pullovers, which are knitted in a cable and bobble pattern, to give some richly elaborate effects. When it comes to embroidering the flowers, you can obviously use any color of yarn you like or match it with something to make an outfit.

Louisa's Sweater

Shown on page 72, right

MEASUREMENTS

To fit approx age 6 mths (2 yrs:4 yrs).
Actual chest measurement 48(58.5:63.5)cm
[19(23:25)in].
Length 25.5(31.5:35.5)cm [10(12^1/$_2$:14)in].
Sleeve seam approx 19(23:28)cm [7^1/$_2$(9:11)in].

MATERIALS

Rowan Lightweight DK 25g hanks; Main color MC
7(8:9) hanks, small amounts of 2 contrasting colors, A
and B, for embroidery.
1 pair each of 2^1/$_4$mm (size 1) and 3mm (size 2) knitting
needles.
Cable needle.

GAUGE

28 sts and 35 rows to 10cm (4in) square over st st on
3mm (size 2) needles.
Fancy cable measures approx 2cm (^{3}/$_4$in) wide.

SPECIAL ABBREVIATIONS

yb = yarn back.
yo = yarn over needle.
Cr4F = sl next 3 sts onto cable needle and leave at
front of work, P1, then K1, yo, K2 tog from cable
needle.
Cr4B = sl next st onto cable needle and leave at back of
work, sl 1, K1, psso, yo, K1, then P1 from cable
needle.
Cr6F = sl next 3 sts onto cable needle and leave at
front of work, K1, yo, K2 tog, then sl 1, K1, psso, yo,
K1 from cable needle.
Cr4R = sl next st onto cable needle and leave at back of
work, K1, yo, K2 tog, then P1 from cable needle.
Cr4L = sl next 3 sts onto cable needle and leave at
front of work, P1, then yb, sl 1, K1, psso, yo, K1 from
cable needle.
MB = [P1, K1, P1 and K1] all into next st, turn, K4,
turn, P4, sl 2nd, 3rd and 4th sts over first st.

BACK

With 2^1/$_4$mm (size 1) needles and MC, cast on 64(80:88)
sts.
Work in K1, P1 rib for 4(5:5)cm [1^1/$_2$(2:2)in] inc to
72(88:96) sts in last row.
Change to 3mm (size 2) needles.
Work in patt as follows:
ROW 1 (right side) P11(15:17), K1, yo, K2 tog, P2, yb,
sl 1, K1, psso, yo, K1, * P13(17:19), K1, yo, K2 tog,
P2, yb, sl 1, K1, psso, yo, K1; rep from * to last
11(15:17) sts, P11(15:17).
ROW 2 K11(15:17), P3, K2, P3, * K13(17:19), P3, K2,
P3; rep from * to last 11(15:17) sts, K11(15:17).
ROWS 3 AND 4 As rows 1 and 2.
ROW 5 P11(15:17), Cr4F, Cr4B, * P13(17:19), Cr4F,
Cr4B; rep from * to last 11(15:17) sts, P11(15:17).

ROW 6 K12(16:18), P6, * K15(19:21), P6; rep from * to
last 12(16:18) sts, K12(16:18).
ROW 7 P4(6:7), MB, * P7(9:10), Cr6F, P7(9:10), MB;
rep from * to last 4(6:7) sts, P4(6:7).
ROW 8 As row 6.
ROW 9 P11(15:17), Cr4R, Cr4L, * P13(17:19), Cr4R,
Cr4L; rep from * to last 11(15:17) sts, P11(15:17).
ROW 10 As row 2. **ROWS 11 AND 12** As rows 1 and 2.
These 12 rows form the patt.
Cont in patt until back measures 15(20.5:23)cm
[6(8:9)in], ending wrong side row.

Shape armholes. Keeping patt correct, bind off
3(4:4) sts at beg of next 2 rows. Dec one st each end of
every row to 58(68:76) sts.
Work straight until armholes measure 10(11.5:12.5)cm
[4(4^1/$_2$:5)in], ending wrong side row.

Shape shoulders. Bind off 7(9:10) sts at beg of next 2
rows, then 6(8:10) sts at beg of foll 2 rows.
Leave rem 32(34:36) sts on a holder.

FRONT

Work as given for back until front measures 10(10:12)
rows **less** than back to beg of shoulder shaping, ending
wrong side row.

Shape neck. **NEXT ROW** Patt 23(27:31), turn and leave
rem sts on a spare needle.
Keeping patt correct, bind off 2 sts at neck edge on
next and foll alt row. Dec one st at neck edge on every
row to 13(17:20) sts.
Work 0(0:1) row straight, ending armhole edge.
Shape shoulder. Bind off 7(9:10) sts at beg of next
row. Work 1 row. Bind off.
With right side facing sl center 12(14:14) sts on a
holder, join yarn to rem sts, patt to end. Work 1 row.
Complete to match first side.

SLEEVES

With 2^1/$_4$mm (size 1) needles and MC, cast on 34(38:46)
sts. Work in K1, P1 rib for 4(5:5)cm [1^1/$_2$(2:2)in].
Change to 3mm (size 2) needles.
Work in patt as follows:
ROW 1 (right side) P13(15:19), K1, yo, K2 tog, P2, yb,
sl 1, K1, psso, yo, K1, P13(15:19).
ROW 2 K13(15:19), P3, K2, P3, K13(15:19).
Cont in patt as set, working as back, AT THE SAME
TIME, inc one st each end of next, then every foll
4th(3rd:4th) row to 42(48:50) sts, then every foll
5th(4th:5th) row to 54(68:76) sts, working inc sts in
patt, but if there is not enough sts for a complete cable,
work these sts in reverse st st.
Work straight until sleeve measures approx
19(23:28)cm [7^1/$_2$(9:11)in], ending wrong side row and
same patt row as back to beg of armhole shaping.

Shape top. Keeping patt correct, bind off 3(4:4) sts at
beg of next 2 rows.
Dec one st each end of every row to 42(54:62) sts, then

every foll alt row to 36(46:50) sts, then on every row to 18(24:24) sts. Bind off 2(3:3) sts at beg of next 4 rows. Bind off.

NECKBAND
Join right shoulder seam.
With 2¼mm (size 1) needles, right side facing and MC, pick up 16(17:18) sts down left front neck, K front neck sts inc 2 sts, pick up 16(17:18) sts up right front neck, then K back neck sts inc 4 sts. 82(88:92) sts.
Work in K1, P1 rib for 1.5cm (½in).
With 3mm (size 2) needles, bind off loosely in rib.

TO MAKE UP
Around every other bobble, embroider 4 petals in lazy daisy stitch using A, then 4 leaves in straight stitch using B. On remaining bobbles embroider a small French knot using A. Fasten off each flower and knot as worked: do not strand from one place to another.
Join left shoulder and neckband seam. Set in sleeves.
Join side and sleeve seams.

Octavia's Vest

MEASUREMENTS
To fit approx age 6 mths (2 yrs:4 yrs).
Actual chest measurement 45(56:62)cm [17¾(22:24½)in].
Length 23.5(29:33)cm [9¼(11½:13)in] from top of shoulder to bottom of back.

MATERIALS
Rowan Lightweight Double Knitting 25g hanks; Main color MC 5(6:7) hanks, small amounts in 2 contrasting colors, A and B, for embroidery.
1 pair each of 2¼mm (size 1) and 3mm (size 2) knitting needles.
Cable needle.
4(5:5) small buttons.

GAUGE
28 sts and 35 rows to 10cm (4in) square over st st on 3mm (size 2) needles.
Fancy cable measures approx 2cm (¾in) wide.

SPECIAL ABBREVIATIONS
yb = yarn back.
yo = yarn over needle.
Cr4F = slip next 3 sts onto cable needle and leave at front of work, P1, then K1, yo, K2 tog from cable needle.
Cr4B = sl next st onto cable needle and leave at back of work, sl 1, K1, psso, yo, K1, then P1 from cable needle.
Cr6F = sl next 3 sts onto cable needle and leave at front of work, K1, yo, K2 tog, then sl 1, K1, psso, yo, K1 from cable needle.
Cr4R = sl next st onto cable needle and leave at back of work, K1, yo, K2 tog, then P1 from cable needle.
Cr4L = sl next 3 sts onto cable needle and leave at front of work, P 1, then yb, sl 1, K1, psso, yo, K1 from cable needle.
MB = [P1, K1, P1 and K1] all into next st, turn, K4, turn, P4, sl 2nd, 3rd and 4th sts over first st.
pw = purlwise.
kw = knitwise.

BACK
With 2¼mm (size 1) needles and MC, cast on 68(84:92) sts. **ROW 1** (right side) [K1, P1] to end.
ROW 2 [P1, K1] to end.
Rep these 2 rows for seed st patt for 1.5cm (½in).
Change to 3mm (size 2) needles.
Cont in seed st until waistband measures 2cm (¾in), ending wrong side row.
Now work in patt as follows:
ROW 1 (right side) P9(13:15), K1, yo, K2 tog, P2, yb, sl 1, K1, psso, yo, K1, * P13(17:19), k1, yo, K2 tog, P2, yb, sl 1, K1, psso, yo, K1; rep from * to last 9(13:15) sts, P9(13:15).
ROW 2 K9(13:15), P3, K2, P3, * K13(17:19), P3, K2, P3; rep from * to last 9(13:15) sts, K9(13:15).
ROWS 3 AND 4 As rows 1 and 2.
ROW 5 P9(13:15), Cr4F, Cr4B, * P13(17:19), Cr4F, Cr4B; rep from * to last 9(13:15) sts, P9(13:15).
ROW 6 K10(14:16), P6, * K15(19:21), P6; rep from * to last 10(14:16) sts, K10(14:16).
ROW 7 P2(4:5), MB, * P7(9:10), Cr6F, P7(9:10), MB; rep from * to last 2(4:5) sts, P2(4:5).
ROW 8 As row 6.

OCTAVIA IN HER VEST AND LOUISA IN HER PULLOVER, BOTH KNITS WITH DAISY-EMBROIDERED BOBBLES

ROW 9 P9(13:15), Cr4R, Cr4L, * P13(17:19), Cr4R, Cr4L; rep from * to last 9(13:15) sts, P9(13:15).
ROW 10 As row 2.
ROWS 11 AND 12 As rows 1 and 2.
These 12 rows form the patt.
Cont in patt until back measures 13.5(18:20.5)cm [5$\frac{1}{4}$(7:8)in], ending wrong side row.

Shape armholes. Keeping patt correct, bind off 3(4:4) sts at beg of next 2 rows. Dec one st each end of every row to 54(64:72) sts.
Work straight until armholes measure 10(11.5:12.5)cm [4(4$\frac{1}{2}$:5)in], ending wrong side row.

Shape shoulders. Bind off 6(8:9) sts at beg of next 2

NEXT ROW Cast on 5(5:6) sts and work as follows: P8(8:9), inc pw in last st.
NEXT ROW Inc kw in first st, K9(9:10).

<u>**2nd and 3rd sizes only.**</u> **NEXT ROW** Cast on 5 sts and work as follows: K3, P(12:13), inc pw in last st.
NEXT ROW Inc kw in first st, K(13:14), P3.
NEXT ROW Cast on 5 sts and work as follows: P1, K6, P(9:10), MB, P5, inc pw in last st.
NEXT ROW Inc kw in first st, K(16:17), P6, K1.
NEXT ROW Cast on 5 sts and work as follows: P5, Cr4R, Cr4L, P17, inc pw in last (0:1) st.

<u>**1st size only.**</u> **NEXT ROW** Cast on 5 sts and work as follows: P2, K3, P6, MB, P3, inc pw in last st.
NEXT ROW Inc kw in first st, K11, P3, K2.
NEXT ROW Cast on 4 sts and work as follows: P1, K3, P2, yb, sl 1, K1, psso, yo, K1, P13.

<u>**All sizes.**</u> **NEXT ROW** K13(17:19), P3, K2, P3, K1(5:5).
NEXT ROW Cast on 4(4:5) sts and work as follows: P5(9:10), K1, yo, K2 tog, P2, yb, sl 1, K1, psso, yo, K1, P13(17:19).
NEXT ROW K13(17:19), P3, K2, P3, K5(9:10).
NEXT ROW Cast on 4(4:5) sts and work as follows: P9(13:15), K1, yo, K2 tog, P2, yb, sl 1, K1, psso, yo, K1, P13(17:19). 30(38:42) sts.
The last row sets row 1 of patt.
Cont in patt as set, working as back and introducing bobbles in side sts when necessary. Work straight until straight edge of left front side seam measures same as back to beg of armhole shaping (omitting seed st waistband), ending at side edge.

<u>**Shape armhole and front neck.**</u> Keeping patt correct, bind off 3(4:4) sts at beg of next row.
Work 1 row (omit this row when working right front).
Dec one st at front edge on next and every foll alt row, AT THE SAME TIME, dec one st at armhole edge on every row to 21(25:29) sts.
Keeping armhole edge straight, cont to dec at front edge on every foll alt row from last dec to 15(22:26) sts, then on every foll 3rd row to 11(15:18) sts.
Work a few rows straight until front measures same as back to beg of shoulder shaping, ending armhole edge.

<u>**Shape shoulder.**</u> Bind off 6(8:9) sts at beg of next row. Work 1 row. Bind off.

R I G H T   F R O N T

With 3mm (size 2) needles and MC, cast on 3 sts.
NEXT ROW (right side) P3.
NEXT ROW K2, inc kw in last st.
NEXT ROW Inc pw in first st, P3.
NEXT ROW Bind on 5(5:6) sts and work as follows: P9(9:10), inc kw in last st.

<u>**2nd and 3rd sizes only.**</u> **NEXT ROW** Inc pw in first st, P(10:11).

rows, then 5(7:9) sts at beg of foll 2 rows. Bind off rem sts.

L E F T   F R O N T

With 3mm (size 2) needles and MC, cast on 3 sts.
NEXT ROW (right side) P3.
NEXT ROW Inc kw in first st, K2.

NEXT ROW Cast on 5 sts and work as follows: P2, K(14:15), inc kw in last st.
NEXT ROW Inc pw in first st, P5, MB, P(9:10), K2.
NEXT ROW Cast on 5 sts and work as follows: K1, P6, K(16:17), inc kw in last st.
NEXT ROW Inc pw in first (0:1) st, P17, Cr4R, Cr4L.

1st size only. **NEXT ROW** Inc pw in first st, P3, MB, P6. **NEXT ROW** Cast on 5 sts and work as follows: K2, P3, K11, inc kw in last st. **NEXT ROW** P13, K3, P2.

All sizes. **NEXT ROW** Cast on 4(5:5) sts and work as follows: K1(5:5), P3, K2, P3, K13(17:19).
NEXT ROW P13(17:19), K1, yo, K2 tog, P2, yb, sl 1, K1, psso, yo, K1, P1(5:5).
NEXT ROW Cast on 4(4:5) sts and work as follows: K5(9:10), P3, K2, P3, K13(17:19).
NEXT ROW P13(17:19), K1, yo, K2 tog, P2, yb, sl 1, K1, psso, yo, K1, P5(9:10).
NEXT ROW Cast on 4(4:5) sts and work as follows: K9(13:15), P3, K2, P3, K13(17:19). 30(38:42) sts.
The last row sets row 2 of patt.
Cont as left front, noting exception in parentheses.

FRONT BOTTOM EDGING AND BUTTON BAND
Join shoulder seams.
With 2¼mm (size 1) needles and MC, cast on 6 sts. Work in seed st as given for back waistband until band, slightly stretched, measures same from side seam of front to inner edge of point, ending outer edge.
Work mitered corner as follows:
*NEXT 2 ROWS Patt 2, turn, sl 1, patt 1.
NEXT 2 ROWS Patt 3, turn, sl 1, patt to end.
NEXT 2 ROWS Patt 4, turn, sl 1, patt to end.
NEXT 2 ROWS Patt 5, turn, sl 1, patt to end *.
Work straight across all sts until band, slightly stretched, measures from point to beg of straight front edge, ending outer edge.
Rep from * to * for 2nd mitered corner.
Work straight across all sts until band, slightly stretched, fits up front edge and across to center back neck. Bind off in patt.
Sew edging and band in place. Mark positions on band for 4(5:5) buttons, first at top of 2nd mitered corner, last at beg of neck shaping and rem evenly spaced between.

FRONT BOTTOM EDGING AND BUTTONHOLE BAND
Work as given for front bottom edging and button band, reversing shaping and making buttonholes to match markers as follows:
BUTTONHOLE ROW 1 (right side) Patt 2, bind off 2, patt to end. **BUTTONHOLE ROW 2** Patt, casting on 2 sts over those bound off.

ARMHOLE BANDS
With 2¼mm (size 1) needles, right side facing and MC, pick up 70(80:86) sts around armhole edge.

Work in seed st as given for back waistband for 1.5cm (½in), dec one st each end of every row. Bind off in patt.

TO MAKE UP
Around every other bobble embroider 4 petals in lazy daisy stitch using A, then 4 leaves in straight stitch using B. On remaining bobbles, embroider a small French knot using A. Fasten off each flower and knot as worked. Join side and armhole band seams. Join bands at center back neck. Sew on buttons.

Antonia's Cardigan
Shown on page 68

MEASUREMENTS
To fit approx age 6 mths (2 yrs:4 yrs).
Actual chest measurement 50(60.5:66)cm [19¾(23¾:26)in].
Length 25.5(31.5:35.5)cm [10(12½:14)in].
Sleeve seam 19(23:28)cm [7½(9:11)in].

MATERIALS
Rowan Lightweight DK 25g hanks; Main color (MC) 8(10:12) hanks, small amounts in 2 contrasting colors, A and B, for embroidery.
1 pair each of 2¼mm (size 1) and 3mm (size 2) knitting needles. Cable needle. 6(7:8) small buttons.

GAUGE
28 sts and 35 rows to 10cm (4in) square over st st on 3mm (size 2) needles.
Fancy cable measures approx 2cm (¾in) wide.

SPECIAL ABBREVIATIONS
yb = yarn back.
yo = yarn over needle
Cr4F = sl next 3 sts onto cable needle and leave at front of work, P1, then K1, yo, K2 tog from cable needle.
Cr4B = sl next st onto cable needle and leave at back of work, sl 1, K1, psso, yo, K1, then P1 from cable needle.
Cr6F = sl next 3 sts onto cable needle and leave at front of work, K1, yo, K2 tog, then sl 1, K1, psso, yo, K1 from cable needle.
Cr4R = sl next st onto cable needle and leave at back of work, K1, yo, K2 tog, then P1 from cable needle.
Cr4L = sl next 3 sts onto cable needle and leave at front of work, P 1, then yb, sl 1, K1, psso, yo, K1 from cable needle.
MB = [P1, K1, P1 and K1] all into next st, turn, K4, turn, P4, sl 2nd, 3rd and 4th sts over first st.

BACK
With 2¼mm (size 1) needles and MC, cast on 64(80:88) sts. Work in K1, P1 rib for 4(5:5)cm [1½(2:2)in] inc to 72(88:96) sts in last row.

Change to 3mm (size 2) needles.
Work in patt as follows:
ROW 1 (right side) P11(15:17), K1, yo, K2 tog, P2, yb, sl 1, K1, psso, yo, K1, * P13(17:19), K1, yo, K2 tog, P2, yb, sl 1, K1, psso, yo, K1; rep from * to last 11(15:17) sts, P11(15:17).
ROW 2 K11(15:17), P3, K2, P3, * K13(17:19), P3, K2, P3; rep from * to last 11(15:17) sts, K11(15:17).
ROWS 3 AND 4 As rows 1 and 2.
ROW 5 P11(15:17), Cr4F, Cr4B, * P13(17:19), Cr4F, Cr4B; rep from * to last 11(15:17) sts, P11(15:17).
ROW 6 K12(16:18), P6, * K15(19:21), P6; rep from * to last 12(16:18) sts, K12(16:18).
ROW 7 P4(6:7), MB, * P7(9:10), Cr6F, P7(9:10), MB; rep from * to last 4(6:7) sts, P4(6:7).
ROW 8 As row 6.
ROW 9 P11(15:17), Cr4R, Cr4L, * P13(17:19), Cr4R, Cr4L; rep from * to last 11(15:17) sts, P11(15:17).
ROW 10 As row 2. ROWS 11 AND 12 As rows 1 and 2.
These 12 rows form the patt.
Cont in patt until back measures 15(20.5:23)cm [6(8:9)in], ending wrong side row.

Shape armholes. Keeping patt correct, bind off 3(4:4) sts at beg of next 2 rows. Dec one st each end of every row to 58(68:76) sts.
Work straight until armholes measure 10(11.5:12.5)cm [4(4$\frac{1}{2}$:5)in], ending wrong side row.
Shape shoulders. Bind off 7(9:10) sts at beg of next 2 rows, then 6(8:10) sts at beg of foll 2 rows. Leave rem 32(34:36) sts on a holder.

LEFT FRONT
With 2$\frac{1}{4}$mm (size 1) needles cast on 30(38:42) sts.
Work in K1, P1 rib for 4(5:5)cm [1$\frac{1}{2}$(2:2)in] inc to 34(42:46) sts in last row.
Change to 3mm (size 2) needles.
ROW 1 (right side) P11(15:17), K1, yo, K2 tog, P2, yb, sl 1, k1, psso, yo, K1, P15(19:21).
ROW 2 K15(19:21), P3, K2, P3, K11(15:17).
Cont in patt as set, working as back until front measures same as back to beg of armhole shaping, ending wrong side row (for right front end right side row here).

Shape armhole. Keeping patt correct, bind off 3(4:4) sts at beg of next row.
Work 1 row (for right front omit this row).
Dec one st at armhole edge on every row to 27(32:36) sts.
Work straight until front measures 10(10:12) rows (for right front read 9(9:11) rows here) **less** than back to beg of shoulder shaping, ending armhole edge.

Shape neck. NEXT ROW Patt 23(27:31), turn and leave rem sts on a spare needle.
Bind off 2 sts at neck edge on next and foll alt row. Dec one st at neck edge on every row to 13(17:20) sts.
Work 0(0:1) row straight, ending armhole edge.

Shape shoulder. Bind off 7(9:10) sts at beg of next row. Work 1 row. Bind off.

RIGHT FRONT
Work as given for left front, noting exception in parentheses and set patt as follows:
ROW 1 (right side) P15(19:21), K1, yo, K2 tog, P2, yb, sl 1, K1, psso, yo, K1, P11(15:17).
ROW 2 K11(15:17), P3, K2, P3, K15(19:21).

SLEEVES
Work as given for sleeves of Louisa's sweater (page 70).

BUTTON BAND
With 2$\frac{1}{4}$mm (size 1) needles and MC, cast on 11 sts.
Beg alt rows P1, work in K1, P1 rib until band, slightly stretched, fits up front to beg of neck shaping. Leave sts on a holder. Sew band in place. Mark positions on band for 6(7:8) buttons, first and last approx 1.5cm ($\frac{1}{2}$in) from bind-on edge and holder and rem evenly spaced between.

BUTTONHOLE BAND
Work as given for button band making buttonholes to match markers as follows:
BUTTONHOLE ROW 1 (right side) Rib 4, bind off 3, rib to end. BUTTONHOLE ROW 2 Rib, binding on 3 sts over those bound off.

NECKBAND
Join shoulder seams.
With 2$\frac{1}{4}$mm (size 1) needles, right side facing and MC, bind off in rib first 6 sts of buttonhole band, then rib to end of band, K right front neck sts inc one st, pick up 15(17:18) sts up right front neck, K back neck sts inc 5(7:5) sts, pick up 15(17:18) sts down left front neck, K left front neck sts inc one st, then rib across button band, binding off last 6 sts. 87(97:99) sts.
With wrong side facing, rejoin yarn to rem sts and work 3 rows in rib as set for front bands.
EYELET ROW (right side) [K1, P1] 1(0:1) time, * K1, P1, yo, K2 tog, K1, P1; rep from * to last st, K1.
Rib another 3 rows.
Bind off to form picot edge as follows: * bind on 2 sts, P1, [P1, sl second st on right-hand needle over first st] 4 times, sl rem st on right-hand needle back to left-hand needle; rep from * to last st, fasten off.

TO MAKE UP
Around every other bobble, embroider 4 petals in lazy daisy stitch using A, then 4 leaves in straight stitch using B. On remaining bobbles, embroider a small French knot using A (if desired). Fasten off each flower and knot as worked; do not strand from one place to another. Set in sleeves. Join side and sleeve seams. Sew on buttons. With MC, make a twisted cord and thread through eyelet holes at neck. Attach a tassel to each end of cord.

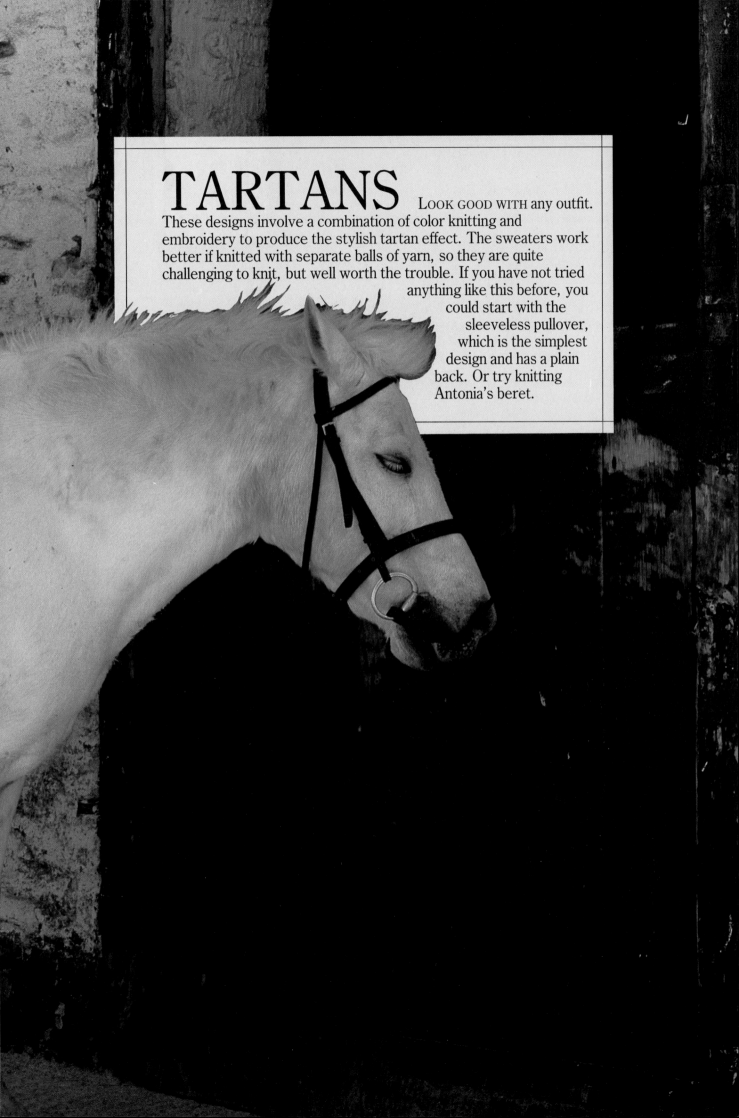

TARTANS

LOOK GOOD WITH any outfit. These designs involve a combination of color knitting and embroidery to produce the stylish tartan effect. The sweaters work better if knitted with separate balls of yarn, so they are quite challenging to knit, but well worth the trouble. If you have not tried anything like this before, you could start with the sleeveless pullover, which is the simplest design and has a plain back. Or try knitting Antonia's beret.

Antonia's Pullover

MEASUREMENTS
To fit approx age 6 mths (2 yrs:4 yrs).
Actual chest measurement 48(58.5:63.5)cm [19(23:25)in].
Length 25.5(31.5:35.5)cm [10(12$\frac{1}{2}$:14)in].
Sleeve seam 19(23:28)cm [7$\frac{1}{2}$(9:11)in].

MATERIALS
Rowan Lightweight DK 25g hanks; Main color (MC) Black (62) 6(7:8) hanks, 1st contrasting color (A) Red (115) 1(2:2) hanks, 2nd contrasting color (B) White (01) 1(1:1) hank, 3rd contrasting color (C) Blue (55) 1(1:1) hank. 1 pair each of 2$\frac{3}{4}$mm (size 2) and 3$\frac{1}{4}$mm (size 3) knitting needles. 1 each of 2$\frac{3}{4}$mm (size 2) and 3$\frac{1}{4}$mm (size 3) set of 4 double-pointed knitting needles.

GAUGE
28 sts and 30 rows to 10cm (4in) square over patt on 3$\frac{1}{4}$mm (size 3) needles.

Note When working patt from chart strand yarn not in use loosely across back of work over no more than 3 sts at a time, making sure that the same gauge is obtained throughout.

BACK
With 2$\frac{3}{4}$mm (size 2) needles and MC, cast on 54(68:74) sts.
Work in K1, P1 rib for 4(5:5)cm [1$\frac{1}{2}$(2:2)in] inc to 67(81:87) sts in last row.
Change to 3$\frac{1}{4}$mm (size 3) needles.
Beg K row, work in st st from chart 1 (page 81) following markers for back until back measures approx 15(20.5:23)cm [6(8:9)in], ending patt row 4(14:24).

Shape armholes. Keeping patt correct, bind off 3(4:4) sts at beg of next 2 rows.
Dec one st each end of every row to 53(63:69) sts.
Work straight until armholes measure 10(11.5:12.5)cm [4(4$\frac{1}{2}$:5)in], ending P row.

Shape shoulders. Bind off 6(8:9) sts at beg of next 2 rows, then 5(7:8) sts at beg of foll 2 rows. Leave rem sts on a holder.

FRONT
Work as given for back, following markers for front, until front measures 8(8:10) rows **less** than back to beg of shoulder shaping, ending P row.

Shape neck. NEXT ROW Patt 21(25:28), turn and leave rem sts on a spare needle.
Keeping patt correct, bind off 3 sts at neck edge on next and foll alt row. Dec one st at neck edge on every row to 11(15:17) sts.
Work 0(0:1) row straight, ending armhole edge.

Shape shoulder. Bind off 6(8:9) sts at beg of next row. Work 1 row. Bind off.
With right side facing sl center 11(13:13) sts on a holder, join yarn to rem sts and patt to end. Work 1 row. Complete to match first side.

SLEEVES
With 2$\frac{3}{4}$mm (size 2) needles and MC, cast on 32(34:40) sts.
Work in K1, P1 rib for 4(5:5)cm [1$\frac{1}{2}$(2:2)in] inc to 35(35:41) sts in last row.
Change to 3$\frac{1}{4}$mm (size 3) needles.
Beg K row and patt row 21(21:17) and work in st st from of chart 1 following markers for sleeves, inc one st each end of every 5th(3rd:3rd) row to 43(59:45) sts, then every foll 6th(4th:4th) row to 49(63:71) sts, working inc sts in patt.
Work straight until sleeve measures approx 19(23:28)cm [7$\frac{1}{2}$(9:11)in], ending patt row 4(14:24).

Shape top. Keeping patt correct, bind off 3(4:4) sts at beg of next 2 rows. Dec one st each end of every row to 37(45:53) sts, then every foll alt row to 33(41:47) sts, then every row to 23(27:29) sts. Bind off 3(3:4) sts at beg of next 2 rows, then 3(4:4) sts at beg of foll 2 rows. Bind off.

COLLAR
Join shoulder seams.
With 2$\frac{3}{4}$mm (size 2) set of 4 needles, right side facing and MC, sl first 5(6:6) sts of center front neck onto another holder, K rem front neck sts from holder, pick up 16(16:18) sts up right front neck, K back neck sts inc 4 sts, pick up 16(16:18) sts down left front neck, inc one st, then K front neck sts from holder. 79(83:89) sts. Turn.
Work backwards and forwards in rows of rib as follows: Beg alt rows P1, work in K1, P1 rib for 2.5cm (1in).
Change to 3$\frac{1}{4}$mm (size 3) set of 4 needles and cont in rib as set until collar measures 5(5.5:6.5)cm [2(2$\frac{1}{4}$:2$\frac{1}{2}$)in]. Bind off loosely in rib.

TO MAKE UP
Set in sleeves. Join side and sleeve seams. At center-front, catch-stitch together first two sts at base of collar to prevent neck from gaping.

•

ANTONIA'S BERET WITH ITS LARGE-SIZED POMPOM MATCHES HER PULLOVER

Matching Beret

MEASUREMENT
To suit approx age 6 mths (2 to 4 yrs)

MATERIALS
Rowan Lightweight Double Knitting 25g hanks;
Main color (MC) Black (62) 2(2) hanks; small amounts
of 3 contrasting colors in (A) red (115), (B) white (1)
and (C) blue (55) for duplicate stitch and pompom.
1 pair of 3mm (size 2) knitting needles.

GAUGE
28 sts and 35 rows to 10cm (4in) square over st st on
3mm (size 2) needles.

SPECIAL ABBREVIATION
kw = knitwise

With 3mm (size 2) needles and MC, bind on 94(139)
sts.
NEXT ROW (right side) K3, * inc kw in next st, K9(14);
rep from * to last st, K1.
NEXT AND EVERY FOLL ALT ROW P.
NEXT ROW K3, * inc kw in next st, K10(15); rep from *
to last st, K1.
NEXT ROW K3, * inc kw in next st, K11(16); rep from *
to last st, K1.
NEXT ROW K3, * inc kw in next st, K12(17); rep from *
to last st, K1.
NEXT ROW K3, * inc kw in next st, K13(18); rep from *
to last st, K1.

NEXT ROW K3, * inc kw in next st, K14(19); rep from *
to last st, K1.
2ND SIZE ONLY. NEXT ROW K3, * inc kw in next st, K20;
rep from * to last st, K1.
BOTH SIZES. NEXT ROW P. 148(202) sts.

Shape crown. NEXT ROW K3, * sl 1, K1, psso,
K14(20); rep from * to last st, K1.
NEXT AND EVERY FOLL ALT ROW P.
NEXT ROW K3, * sl 1, K1, psso, K13(19); rep from * to
last st, K1.
NEXT ROW K3, * sl 1, K1, psso, K12(18); rep from * to
last st, K1.
Cont to dec as set working one st less in each rep to 22
sts.
NEXT ROW P.
NEXT ROW [Sl 1, K1, psso] to end. 11 sts
Break off yarn leaving an end. Run end through rem
sts, draw up tightly and secure.

RIBBING
With 3mm (size 2) needles, right side facing and MC,
pick up 70(110) sts from bind-on edge.
Work in K1, P1 rib for 10 rows.
Bind off loosely in rib.

DUPLICATE STITCH

Half-embroidered tartan beret. Beg on row 1 of
st st, above rib, and following chart for half-
embroidered tartan beret, duplicate stitch the 11 st
motif 9 times around beret, until the 23 rows have been
worked.

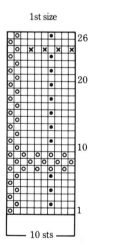

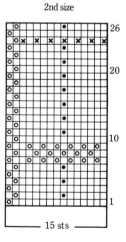

Key
□ = MC
◉ = Swiss embroider in A
◙ = Swiss embroider in B
✕ = Swiss embroider in C

WORK THE BERET PATTERN
FROM THIS CHART AND KEY

●

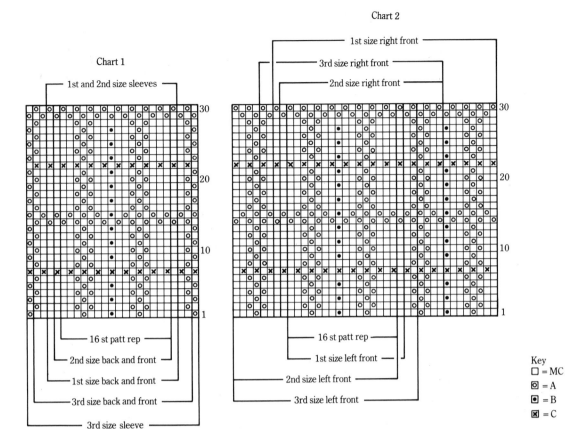

CHARTS FOR ANTONIA'S PULLOVER, ASHLEY'S CARDIGAN, AND EDWARD'S PULLOVER

•

All-over embroidered tartan beret. Beg on row 1 of st st, above rib, and following chart for all-over embroidered tartan beret, and size required, duplicate stitch the motif around beret, adding and subtracting from side sts as necessary and repeating the motif as required until center of beret has been reached.

TO MAKE UP
Join back seam. Make a pompom using all colors, and attach to top of beret. If necessary, run a few rows of shirring elastic through ribbing to give a firmer fit.

Laura's Vest
Shown on page 83, left

MEASUREMENTS
To fit approx age 2 yrs (4 yrs).
Actual chest measurement 57(61.5)cm [22¹/₂(24¹/₂)in].
Length 29(33)cm [11¹/₂(13)in] from shoulder to base of back.

MATERIALS
Rowan Lightweight DK 25g hanks; Main color (MC) Red (115) 5(6) hanks, 1st contrasting color (A) Green (606) 1(1) hank, 2nd contrasting color (B) White (1) 1(1) hank, 3rd contrasting color (C) Yellow (12) 1(1) hank. 1 pair each of 2³/₄mm (size 2) and 3¹/₄mm (size 3) knitting needles.
5 buttons.

GAUGE
28 sts and 30 rows to 10cm (4in) square over patt on 3¹/₄mm (size 3) needles.

SPECIAL ABBREVIATIONS
pw = purlwise.
kw = knitwise.

Note When working patt from chart strand yarn not in use loosely across back of work over no more than 3 sts at a time, making sure that the same gauge is obtained throughout.

BACK
With 2³/₄mm (size 2) needles and MC, cast on 79(85) sts.
SEED ST ROW K1, [P1, K1] to end.
Rep this row for 1.5cm (¹/₂in).
Change to 3¹/₄mm (size 3) needles.
Cont in seed st until waistband measures 2cm (³/₄in).
Beg K row, work in st st from chart following markers for back until back measures approx 18(20.5)cm

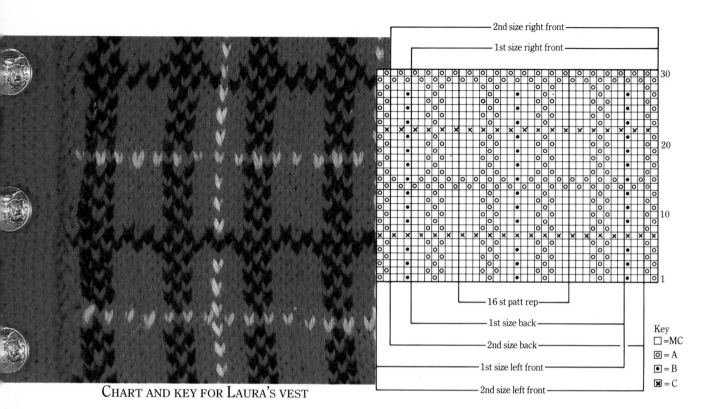

CHART AND KEY FOR LAURA'S VEST

•

[7(8)in], ending patt row 18(24).

Shape armholes. Keeping patt correct, bind off 5 sts at beg of next 2 rows. Dec one st each end of every row to 57(63) sts.
Work straight until armholes measure 11.5(12.5)cm [4½(5)in], ending P row.

Shape shoulders. Bind off 6(8) sts at beg of next 2 rows, then 6(7) sts at beg of foll 2 rows.
Bind off rem sts.

LEFT FRONT
With 3¼mm (size 3) needles and MC, cast on 3 sts.
NEXT ROW K 1MC, 1A, 1MC.
NEXT ROW With A inc pw in first st, P 1MC, 1A.
NEXT ROW With MC cast on 7(8) sts and work as follows: K 0(1)MC, 1A, 7MC, 1A, 1MC, with MC inc kw in last st.
NEXT ROW With MC inc pw in first st, P [1MC, 1A] twice, 5MC, 1A, 1MC, 0(1)A.
NEXT ROW With MC cast on 7 sts and work as follows: K0(1)A, 3MC, 1B, 3MC, 1A, 7MC, 1A, 3MC, with B inc kw in last st.
NEXT ROW With MC inc pw in first st, P 3MC, [1A, 1MC, 1A, 5MC] twice, 1A, 0(1)MC.
NEXT ROW With MC cast on 7 sts and work as follows: K 1(0)A, [1MC, 1A] 13(14) times, 1MC, with A inc kw in last st.
NEXT ROW With A inc pw in first st, P [1MC, 1A] 14(15) times, 1(0)MC.
NEXT ROW With MC cast on 5(7) sts and work as

follows: K 0(2)MC, 0(1)B, 3MC, 1A, 7MC, 1A, 3MC, 1B, 3MC, 1A, 7MC, 1A, 3MC, 1B, 3MC, 1A. 36(39) sts.
The last row was row 1 of chart.
Cont in patt as set, working in st st from chart, following markers for left front until straight edge of left front side seam measures same as back to beg of armhole shaping (omitting seed st waistband), ending patt row 18(24). (For right front end patt row 19[25] here.)

Shape armhole and front neck. Keeping patt correct, bind off 5 sts at beg of next row.
Work 1 row (omit this row when working right front).
Dec one st at front edge on next and every foll alt row, AT THE SAME TIME, dec one st at armhole edge on every row to 22(25) sts.
Keeping armhole edge straight, cont to dec at front edge on every foll alt row from last dec to 16(21) sts, then on every foll 3rd row to 12(15) sts.
Work a few rows straight until front measures same as back to beg of shoulder shaping, ending armhole edge.

Shape shoulder. Bind off 6(8) sts at beg of next row.
Work 1 row. Bind off.

RIGHT FRONT
With 3¼mm (size 3) needles and MC, cast on 3 sts.
NEXT ROW (right side) K 1MC, 1A, 1MC.
NEXT ROW P 1A, 1MC, with A inc pw in last st.

LAURA IN HER VEST, LITTLE ASHLEY IN HER
CARDIGAN

NEXT ROW With MC inc kw in first st, 1MC, 1A, 1MC.
NEXT ROW With MC cast on 7(8) sts and work as follows: P 0(1)A, 1MC, 1A, 5MC, [1A, 1MC] twice, with MC inc pw in last st.
NEXT ROW With B inc kw in first st, K 3MC, 1A, 7MC, 1A, 0(1) MC.
NEXT ROW With MC cast on 7 sts and work as follows: P 0(1)MC, 1A, [5MC, 1A, 1MC, 1A] twice, 3MC, with MC inc pw in last st.
NEXT ROW With A inc kw in first st, K [1MC, 1A] 10(11) times, 1(0)MC.
NEXT ROW With MC cast on 7 sts and work as follows: P 1(0)MC, [1A, 1MC] 14(15) times, with A inc pw in last st.
NEXT ROW K 1A, 3MC, 1B, 3MC, 1A, 7MC, 1A, 3MC, 1B, 3MC, 1A, 6(7)MC.
NEXT ROW With MC cast on 5(7) sts and work as follows: P 2(5)MC, [1A, 1MC, 1A, 5MC] 4 times, 1A, 1MC. 36(39) sts.
(The last row was row 2 of chart.)
Cont as given for left front, working in st st from chart following markers for right front and noting exceptions in parentheses.

FRONT BOTTOM EDGING AND BUTTON BAND

With 2³/₄mm (size 2) needles and MC, cast on 6 sts.
ROW 1 (right side) [K1, P1] to end.
ROW 2 [P1, K1] to end.
These 2 rows form the seed st patt.
Cont in patt until band, slightly stretched, measures from side seam of front to inner edge of point, ending outer edge.
Work mitered corner as follows:
* **NEXT 2 ROWS** Patt 2, turn, sl 1, patt 1.
NEXT 2 ROWS Patt 3, turn, sl 1, patt to end.
NEXT 2 ROWS Patt 4, turn, sl 1, patt to end.
NEXT 2 ROWS Patt 5, turn, sl 1, patt to end *.
Work straight across all sts until band, slightly stretched, measures from point to beg of straight front edge, ending outer edge.
Rep from * to * for 2nd mitered corner.
Work straight across all sts until band, slightly stretched, fits up front edge to beg of neck shaping, ending at inner edge.

Shape lapel. Inc one st at inner edge on next and every foll alt row to 11(13) sts, working inc sts in patt.
Work straight until lapel measures 7.5(8)cm [3(3¹/₄)in] from beg of incs, ending at straight edge.
Bind off in patt. Sew edging and band in place.
Place markers on band for 5 buttons, first at top of 2nd mitered corner, last at beg of lapel (neck) shaping and rem evenly spaced between.

FRONT BOTTOM EDGING AND BUTTONHOLE BAND

Work as given for front bottom edging and button band reversing shaping and making buttonholes to match markers as follows:

BUTTONHOLE ROW 1 (right side) Patt 2, bind off 2, patt to end.
BUTTONHOLE ROW 2 Patt, casting on 2 sts over those bound off.

ARMHOLE BANDS

Join shoulder seams.
With 2³/₄mm (size 2) needles, right side facing and MC, pick up 79(85) sts around armhole edge.
Work in seed st patt as back waistband for 1.5cm (¹/₂in), dec one st each end of every row. Bind off in patt.

COLLAR

With 2³/₄mm (size 2) needles and MC, cast on 26(28) sts.
Working in seed st as given for button band and keeping patt correct, bind on 5(6) sts at beg of next 4 rows, then 5 sts at beg of foll 2 rows, working inc sts in patt. 56(62) sts.
Cont straight in patt until straight edge of row ends measure 5(5.5)cm [2(2¹/₄)in]. Bind off loosely in patt.

TO MAKE UP

Sew cast-on edge of collar to back neck, beginning and ending at top of front bands. Join bound-off edge of front bands to row ends of collar for 2(2.5)cm [³/₄(1)in] from inner edge, leaving remainder of seam free. Join side and armhole band seams, matching front bands to back waistband. Sew on buttons.

•

Ashley's Cardigan

MEASUREMENTS

To fit approximate age 6 mths(2 yrs:4 yrs).
Actual chest measurement 50(60.5:65.5)cm [19³/₄(23³/₄:25³/₄)in].
Length 25.5(31.5:35.5)cm [10(12¹/₂:14)in].
Sleeve seam 19(23:28)cm [7¹/₂(9:11)in].

MATERIALS

Rowan Lightweight DK 25g hanks. Main color (MC) Red (115) 7(8:9) hanks, 1st contrasting color (A) Green (606) 1(2:2) hanks, 2nd contrasting color (B) White (01) 1(1:1) hank, 3rd contrasting color (C) Yellow (12) 1(1:1) hank. 1 pair each of 2³/₄mm (size 2) and 3¹/₄mm (size 3) knitting needles.
4(4:5) buttons.

GAUGE

28 sts and 30 rows to 10cm (4in) square over patt on 3¹/₄mm (size 3) needles.

Note When working patt from chart strand yarn not in use loosely across back of work over no more than 3 sts at a time, making sure that the same gauge is obtained throughout.

B A C K
Work as back of Antonia's pullover (page 78).

L E F T   F R O N T
With 2³/₄mm (size 2) needles and MC, cast on 26(32:36) sts.
Work in K1, P1 rib for 4(5:5)cm [1¹/₂(2:2)in] inc to 33(40:43) sts in last row.
Change to 3¹/₄mm (size 3) needles.
Beg K row, work in st st from chart 2 (page 81) following markers for left front until front measures approx 12(16.5:19)cm [4³/₄(6¹/₂:7¹/₂)in], ending patt row 24(4:12) (for right front end patt row 25(5:13) here).

Shape neck. Keeping patt correct, dec one st at front edge on next and every foll 3rd row to 29(36:39) sts, ending patt row 4(14:24), (for right front work 1 row more here).

Shape armhole. Bind off 3(4:4) sts at beg of next row.
Work 1 row (for right front omit this row).
Dec one st at front edge as before on every 3rd row from last dec, AT THE SAME TIME, dec one st at armhole edge on every row to 20(25:27) sts.
Keeping armhole edge straight, cont to dec at front edge as before to 16(20:22) sts, then dec at front edge

on every foll alt row to 11(15:17) sts.
Work a few rows straight until front measures same as back to beg of shoulder shaping, ending armhole edge.

Shape shoulder. Bind off 6(8:9) sts at beg of next row. Work 1 row. Bind off.

R I G H T   F R O N T
Work as given for left front, noting exceptions in parentheses and following markers for right front on chart.

S L E E V E S
Work as given for sleeves of Antonia's pullover (page 78).

B U T T O N   B A N D   A N D   C O L L A R
Join shoulder seams.
With 2³/₄mm (size 2) needles and MC, cast on 8(10:10) sts.
ROW 1 (right side) [K1, P1] to end.
ROW 2 [P1, K1] to end.
These 2 rows form the seed st patt.
Cont straight in patt until band, slightly stretched, fits up front to beg of neck shaping, ending wrong side row (for buttonhole band and collar end right side row here).

Shape collar. Keeping patt correct, inc one st at beg (inside edge) of next and every foll 6th row to 15(17:19) sts, working inc sts in patt.
Cont straight until collar measures 10(11.5:12.5)cm [4(4¹/₂:5)in] from beg of shaping ending at straight front edge.
NEXT ROW Bind off 5(6:7) sts, patt to end.
NEXT ROW Patt to end, turn and bind on 6(7:8) sts.
Cont straight until band and collar, slightly stretched, fits up front and across to center back neck. Bind off in patt. Sew band in place.
Mark positions on band for 3(4:5) buttons, first approx 1.5cm (¹/₂in) from beg, last at beg of neck shaping and rem evenly spaced between.

B U T T O N H O L E   B A N D   A N D   C O L L A R
Work as given for button band and collar, noting exception in parentheses and making buttonholes to match markers as follows:
BUTTONHOLE ROW 1 (right side) Patt 3(4:4), bind off 2, patt to end.
BUTTONHOLE ROW 2 Patt, binding on 2 sts over those bound off.

T O   M A K E   U P
Set in sleeves. Join side and sleeve seams. Join bound-off edges of collar together at center back neck. Sew on buttons.

Fabian's Pullover

MEASUREMENTS

To fit approx age 6 mths (2 yrs:4 yrs).
Actual chest measurement 48(58.5:63.5)cm
[19(23:25)in].
Length 30.5(37:40.5)cm [12(14¹/₂:16)in].
Sleeve seam 19(23:28)cm [7¹/₂(9:11)in].

MATERIALS

Rowan Lightweight DK 25g hanks. Main color (MC)
Navy (97) 5(6:7) hanks, 1st contrasting color (A) Green
(91) 1(1:1) hank, 2nd contrasting color (B) Black (62)
1(1:1) hank. 1 pair each of 2³/₄mm (size 2) and 3¹/₄mm
(size 3) knitting needles.

GAUGE

26 sts and 34 rows to 10cm (4in) square over st st on
3¹/₄mm (size 3) needles.
28 sts and 30 rows to 10cm (4in) square over patt on
3¹/₄mm (size 3) needles.

Note When working patt from chart strand yarn not in
use loosely across back of work over no more than 3 sts
at a time, making sure that the same gauge is obtained
throughout.

BACK

With 2³/₄mm (size 2) needles and MC, cast on 54(68:74)
sts.
Work in K1, P1 rib for 4(5:5)cm [1¹/₂(2:2)in] inc to
62(76:82) sts in last row.
Change to 3¹/₄mm (size 3) needles.
Beg K row, work in st st and MC only until back
measures 20.5(25.5:28)cm [8(10:11)in], ending P row.

Shape armholes. Bind off 2(3:3) sts at beg of next 2
rows.
Dec one st each end of every row to 52(62:68) sts.
Work straight until armholes measure 10(11.5:12.5)cm
[4(4¹/₂:5)in]; ending P row.

Shape shoulders. Bind off 6(8:9) sts at beg of next 2
rows, then 5(7:8) sts at beg of foll 2 rows. Leave rem
sts on a holder.

FRONT

With 2³/₄mm (size 2) needles and MC, cast on 54(68:74)
sts.
Work in K1, P1 rib for 4(5:5)cm [1¹/₂(2:2)in] inc to
67(81:87) sts in last row.
Change to 3¹/₄mm (size 3) needles.
Beg K row, work in st st from chart following markers
for front until front measures same as back to beg of
armhole shaping, ending P row.

Shape armholes. Keeping patt correct, bind off
3(4:4) sts at beg of next 2 rows.
Dec one st each end of every row to 53(63:69) sts.

Work straight until armholes measure 7.5(9:10)cm
[3(3¹/₂:4)in], ending P row.

Shape neck. **NEXT ROW** Patt 21(25:28), turn and leave
rem sts on a spare needle.
Bind off 3(3:4) sts at neck edge on next row, then 3 sts
on foll alt row. Dec one st at neck edge on every row to
11(15:17) sts, ending armhole edge.

Shape shoulder. Bind off 6(8:9) sts at beg of next
row. Work 1 row. Bind off.
With right side facing sl center 11(13:13) sts on a
holder, join yarn to rem sts and patt to end. Work 1
row. Complete as first side.

SLEEVES

With 2³/₄mm (size 2) needles and MC, cast on
32(34:40)sts.
Work in K1, P1 rib for 4(5:5)cm [1¹/₂(2:2)in].
Change to 3¹/₄mm (size 3) needles.
Beg K row, work in st st and MC only, inc one st each
end of 3rd, then every foll 5th(4th:5th) row to
46(58:66) sts.
Work straight until sleeve measures 19(23:28)cm
[7¹/₂(9:11)in], ending P row.

Shape top. Bind off 2(3:3) sts at beg of next 2 rows.
Dec one st each end of every row to 36(46:54) sts, then
every foll alt row to 30(38:46) sts, then on every row to
16(20:20) sts. Bind off 2(3:3) sts at beg of next 2 rows,
then 3 sts at beg of foll 2 rows. Bind off.

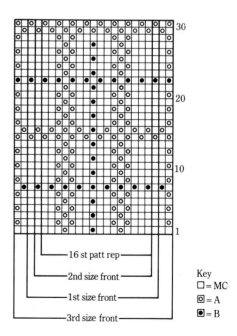

FABIAN'S PULLOVER IS WORKED IN A SUBTLE
THREE-COLOR SCHEME

N E C K B A N D

Join right shoulder seam.

With 2³/₄mm (size 2) needles, right side facing and MC, pick up 16(16:18) sts down left front neck, K front neck sts inc one st, pick up 16(16:18) sts up right front neck, K back neck sts inc 4 sts. 78(82:88) sts.

Work in K1, P1 rib for 1.5cm (¹/₂in). With 3¹/₄mm (size 3) needle, bind off in rib.

T O   M A K E   U P

Join left shoulder and neckband seam. Set in sleeves. Join side and sleeve seams.

•

Edward's Pullover

M E A S U R E M E N T S

To fit approx age 6 mths(2 yrs:4 yrs).
Actual chest measurement 48(58.5:63.5)cm [19(23:25)in].
Length 25.5(31.5:35.5)cm [10(12¹/₂:14)in].

M A T E R I A L S

Rowan Lightweight DK 25g hanks. Main color (MC) Black (62) 4(4:5) hanks, 1st contrasting color (A) Red (115) 1(1:1) hanks, 2nd contrasting color (B) White (01) 1(1:1) hank, 3rd contrasting color (C) Blue (55) 1(1:1) hank.
1 pair each of 2³/₄mm (size 2) and 3¹/₄mm (size 3) knitting needles.

G A U G E

26 sts and 34 rows to 10cm (4in) square over st st on 3¹/₄mm (size 3) needles.
28 sts and 30 rows to 10cm (4in) square over patt on 3¹/₄mm (size 3) needles.

Note When working patt from chart strand yarn not in use loosely across back of work over no more than 3 sts at a time, making sure that the same gauge is obtained throughout.

B A C K

With 2³/₄mm (size 2) needles and MC, cast on 54(68:74) sts.
Work in K1, P1 rib for 4(5:5)cm [1¹/₂(2:2)in] inc to 62(76:82) sts in last row.
Change to 3¹/₄mm (size 3) needles.
Beg K row, work in st st and MC only until back measures 15(20.5:23)cm [6(8:9)in], ending P row.

•

E D W A R D   I N   H I S   S L E E V E L E S S   P U L L O V E R

Shape armholes. Bind off 2(3:3) sts at beg of next 2 rows.
Dec one st each end of every row to 52(62:68) sts.
Work straight until armholes measure 10(11.5:12.5)cm [4(4¹/₂:5)in], ending P row.

Shape shoulders. Bind off 6(8:9) sts at beg of next 2 rows, then 5(7:8) sts at beg of foll 2 rows. Leave rem sts on a holder.

F R O N T

With 2³/₄mm (size 2) needles and MC, cast on 54(68:74) sts.
Work in K1, P1 rib for 4(5:5)cm [1¹/₂(2:2)in] inc to 67(81:87) sts in last row.
Change to 3¹/₄mm (size 3) needles.
Beg K row, work in st st from chart 1 (page 81) following markers for front until front measures same as back to beg of armhole shaping, ending P row.

Shape armholes. Keeping patt correct, bind off 3(4:4) sts at beg of next 2 rows.

Shape neck. NEXT ROW (right side) Work 2 tog, patt next 28(34:37) sts, turn and leave rem sts on a spare needle.
Dec one st at neck edge on next and every row, AT THE SAME TIME dec one st at armhole edge on next 3(4:4) rows. 23(27:30) sts.
Keeping armhole edge straight, cont to dec at neck edge on every row as before to 20(25:28) sts, then on every foll alt row to 11(15:17) sts.
Work a few rows straight until front measures same as back to beg of shoulder shaping, ending armhole edge.

Shape shoulder. Bind off 6(8:9) sts at beg of next row. Work 1 row. Bind off.
With right side facing sl center st on a holder, join yarn to rem sts and patt to last 2 sts, work 2 tog. Complete to match first side, noting exception in parentheses.

N E C K B A N D

Join right shoulder seam. With 2³/₄mm (size 2) needles, right side facing and MC, pick up 28(30:34) sts down left front neck, K center front st and mark this st, pick up 28(30:34) sts up right front neck, then K back neck sts inc 2 sts. 89(95:105) sts.
RIB ROW (wrong side) K1, * P1, K1; rep from * to end.
Cont in rib as set for 1.5cm (¹/₂in), dec one st either side of center marked st on every row. Bind off in rib dec as before.

A R M H O L E   B A N D S

Join left shoulder and neckband seam.
With 2³/₄mm (size 2) needles, right side facing and MC, pick up 70(76:84) sts around armhole edge.
Work in K1, P1 rib for 1.5cm (¹/₂in), dec one st each end of every row. Bind off in rib.

T O   M A K E   U P

Join side and armhole band seams.

COOL COTTONS

MOST OF THE designs in this book lend themselves to being knitted in cotton yarn, so in this chapter, I have selected some from earlier chapters that look equally good in this natural fiber. Nowadays, cotton knitting yarns are available in colors similar to those of wool yarns, so my designs, even the most colorful, have translated beautifully. These sweaters are ideal for a warm day in early autumn or late spring.

Antonia's Cardigan

MEASUREMENTS
To fit approx age 6 mths (2 yrs:4 yrs).
Actual chest measurement 50(60.5:66)cm
[19³/₄(23³/₄:26)in].
Length approx 25.5(31.5:35.5)cm [10(12¹/₂:14)in].
Sleeve seam approx 19(23:28)cm [7¹/₂(9:11)in].

MATERIALS
Rowan Sea Breeze Soft Cotton 50g balls; Main color
(MC) Ecru (522) 2(3:3) balls, 1st contrasting color (A)
Eau-de-Nil (538) 1(1:1) ball, 2nd contrasting color (B)
Wheat (523) 1(1:1) ball, 3rd contrasting color (C) Rain
Cloud (528) 1(1:1) ball, 4th contrasting color (D) Polka
(530) 1(1:1) ball, 5th contrasting color (E) Antique Pink
(533) 1(1:1) ball.
1 pair each of 2mm (size 0) and 2³/₄mm (size 2) knitting
needles.
5(6:6) small buttons.

GAUGE
34 sts and 40 rows to 10cm (4in) square over patt on
2³/₄mm (size 2) needles.

Note When working patt from chart strand yarn not in
use loosely across back of work over no more than 3 sts
at a time, making sure that the same gauge is obtained
throughout.

BACK
With 2mm (size 0) needles and MC, cast on 62(76:82)
sts.
Work in K1, P1 rib for 4(5:5)cm [1¹/₂(2:2)in] inc to
81(97:107) sts in last row.
Change to 2³/₄mm (size 2) needles.
Beg K row, work in st st from chart following markers
for back until back measures approx 15(20.5:23)cm
[6(8:9)in], ending patt row 12(30:8).

Shape armholes. Keeping patt correct, bind off 5 sts
at beg of next 2 rows. Dec one st each end of every row
to 61(75:83) sts.
Work straight until armholes measure 10(11.5:12.5)cm
[4(4¹/₂:5)in], ending P row.

Shape shoulders. Bind off 7(10:11) sts at beg of next
2 rows, then 6(9:11) sts at beg of foll 2 rows.
Leave rem sts on a holder.

LEFT FRONT
With 2mm (size 0) needles and MC, cast on 30(36:40)
sts.
Work in K1, P1 rib for 4(5:5)cm [1¹/₂(2:2)in] inc to
39(47:52) sts in last row.
Change to 2³/₄mm (size 2) needles.
Beg K row, work in st st from chart following markers
for left front until front measures same as back to beg of
armhole shaping, ending patt row 12(30:8) (for right
front end patt row 13(31:9) here).

Shape armhole. Keeping patt correct, bind off 5 sts
at beg of next row.
Work 1 row (omit this row when working right front).
Dec one st at armhole edge on every row to 29(36:40)
sts.
Work straight until armhole measures 10(10:12) rows
(for right front read 9[9:11] rows here) **less** than back
to beg of shoulder shaping, ending armhole edge.

Shape neck. NEXT ROW Patt 25(31:35), turn and leave
rem sts on a holder.
Bind off 3 sts at neck edge on next and foll alt row. Dec
one st at neck edge on every row to 13(19:22) sts.
Work 0(0:1) row straight, ending armhole edge.

Shape shoulder. Bind off 7(10:11) sts at beg of next
row. Work 1 row. Bind off.

RIGHT FRONT
Work as given for left front, noting exceptions in
parentheses and following markers for right front on
chart.

SLEEVES
With 2mm (size 0) needles and MC, cast on 38(46:54)
sts.
Work in K1, P1 rib for 4(5:5)cm [1¹/₂(2:2)in] inc to
41(43:51) sts in last row.
Change to 2³/₄mm (size 2) needles.
Beg K row and patt row 17(23:13) work in st st from

chart following markers for sleeves, inc one st each end
of 5th and every foll 5th(3rd:4th) row to 43(65:69) sts,
then on every foll 6th(4th:5th) row to 59(77:85) sts,
working inc sts in patt.
Work straight until sleeve measures approx
19(23:28)cm [7¹/₂(9:11)in], ending patt row 12(30:8).

Shape top. Keeping patt correct, bind off 5 sts at beg
of next 2 rows. Dec one st each end of every row to
43(57:65) sts, then every foll alt row to 35(49:57) sts,
then every row to 21(27:27) sts. Bind off 3(4:4) sts at
beg of next 4 rows. Bind off.

BUTTON BAND

With 2mm (size 0) needles and MC, cast on 9(9:11) sts.
Beg alt rows P1, work in K1, P1 rib until band, slightly
stretched, fits up front to beg of neck shaping.
Leave sts on a holder. Sew band in place.
Mark positions on band for 4(5:5) buttons, the first
approx 1.5cm (¹/₂in) from bind-on edge, last approx
5(5.5:6.5)cm [2(2¹/₄:2¹/₂)in] from holder and rem evenly
spaced between.

CHART FOR ANTONIA'S CARDIGAN

•

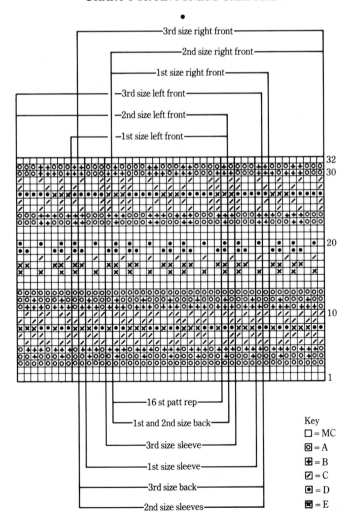

- 3rd size right front
- 2nd size right front
- 1st size right front
- 3rd size left front
- 2nd size left front
- 1st size left front

32
30

20

10

1

- 16 st patt rep
- 1st and 2nd size back
- 3rd size sleeve
- 1st size sleeve
- 3rd size back
- 2nd size sleeves

Key
☐ = MC
◙ = A
⊞ = B
☑ = C
⊡ = D
▨ = E

BUTTONHOLE BAND

Work as given for button band, making buttonholes to
match markers as follows:
BUTTONHOLE ROW 1 (right side) Rib 3(3:4), bind off 3,
rib to end.
BUTTONHOLE ROW 2 Rib, casting on 3 sts over those
bound off.

NECKBAND

Join shoulder seams.
With 2mm (size 0) needles, right side facing and MC,
rib across front band sts, K right front neck sts, pick up
16(16:19) sts up right front neck, K back neck sts inc 4
sts, pick up 16(16:19) sts down left front neck, K left
front neck sts, then rib across front band sts.
97(101:113) sts.
Work in rib as front bands for 1.5cm (¹/₂in), making a
buttonhole as before on rows 2 and 3.
With 2³/₄mm (size 2) needles, bind off in rib.

TO MAKE UP

Set in sleeves. Join side and sleeve seams. Sew on
buttons.

Oliver's Vest

Shown on page 94

MEASUREMENTS

To fit approx age 6 mths (2 yrs:4 yrs).
Actual chest measurement 50(60.5:66)cm
[19³/₄(23³/₄:26)in].
Length approx 25.5(31.5:35.5)cm [10(12¹/₂:14)in].

MATERIALS

Rowan Sea Breeze Soft Cotton 50g balls; Main color
(MC) Polka (530) 1(1:2) ball: 1st contrasting color (A)
Bermuda (539) 1(1:1) ball, 2nd contrasting color (B)
Wheat (B) (523) 1(1:1) ball. 3rd contrasting color (C)
Antique Pink (533) 1(1:1) ball, 4th contrasting color (D)
Rain Cloud (528) 1(1:1) ball, 5th contrasting color (E)
Ecru (522) 1(1:1) ball.
1 pair each of 2mm (size 0) and 2³/₄mm (size 2) knitting
needles.
5(6:6) small buttons.

GAUGE

34 sts and 40 rows to 10cm (4in) square over patt on
2³/₄mm (size 2) needles.

Note When working patt from chart strand yarn not in
use loosely across back of work over no more than 3 sts
at a time, making sure that the same gauge is obtained
throughout.

BACK

With 2mm (size 0) needles and MC, cast on 62(76:82)
sts.
Work in K1, P1 rib for 5(7.5:7.5)cm [2(3:3)in] inc to

81(97:107) sts in last row.
Change to 2³/₄mm (size 2) needles.
Beg K row, work in st st from chart following markers for back until back measures approx 15(20.5:23)cm [6(8:9)in], ending patt row 16(4:14).

Shape armholes. Keeping patt correct, bind off 5 sts at beg of next 2 rows. Dec one st each end of every row to 61(75:83) sts.
Work straight until armholes measure 10(11.5:12.5)cm [4(4¹/₂:5)in], ending P row.

Shape shoulders. Bind off 7(10:11) sts at beg of next 2 rows, then 6(9:11) sts at beg of foll 2 rows. Bind off.

LEFT FRONT
With 2mm (size 0) needles and MC, cast on 30(36:40) sts.
Work in K1, P1 rib for 5(7.5:7.5)cm [2(3:3)in] inc to 39(47:52) sts in last row.
Change to 2³/₄mm (size 2) needles.
Beg K row, work in st st from chart following markers for left front until front measures same as back to beg of armhole shaping, ending patt row 16(4:14), (for right front end patt row 17(5:15) here).

Shape armhole. Keeping patt correct, bind off 5 sts at

beg of next row.
Work 1 row (omit this row when working right front).
Dec one st at armhole on every row to 29(36:40) sts.
Work 1(0:1) row, ending P row.

Shape neck. NEXT ROW Keeping armhole edge straight, dec one st at neck edge on next and every foll alt row to 14(24:25) sts, then every foll 3rd row to 13(19:22) sts, (for right front work 1 row straight here), ending armhole edge.

Shape shoulder. Bind off 7(10:11) sts at beg of next row. Work 1 row. Bind off.

RIGHT FRONT
Work as given for left front, noting exceptions in parentheses and following markers for right front on chart.

BUTTON BAND
Join shoulder seams.
With 2mm (size 0) needles and MC, cast on 9(9:11) sts.
Beg alt rows P1, work in K1, P1 rib until band, slightly stretched, fits front and across to center back neck.
Bind off in rib. Sew band in place. Mark positions on band for 5(6:6) buttons, the first approx 1.5cm (¹/₂in) from bind-on edge, the last at beg of neck shaping and rem evenly spaced between.

BUTTONHOLE BAND
Work as given for button band, making buttonholes to match markers as follows:
BUTTONHOLE ROW 1 (right side) Rib 3(3:4), bind off 3, rib to end.
BUTTONHOLE ROW 2 Rib, casting on 3 sts over those bound off.

ARMHOLE BANDS
With 2mm (size 0) needles, right side facing and MC, pick up 80(86:92) sts around armhole edge.
Work in K1, P1 rib for 1.5cm (¹/₂in) dec one st each end of every row. Bind off in rib.

TO MAKE UP
Join side and armhole band seams. Join bound-off edges of front bands together at center back neck. Sew on buttons.

Elizabeth and Milo's Pullover
Shown on page 96

MEASUREMENTS
To fit approx age 6 mths (2 yrs:4 yrs).
Actual chest measurement 48(58.5:63.5)cm [19(23:25)in].
Length 25.5(31.5:35.5)cm [10(12¹/₂:14)in].
Sleeve seam 19(23:28)cm [7¹/₂(9:11)in].

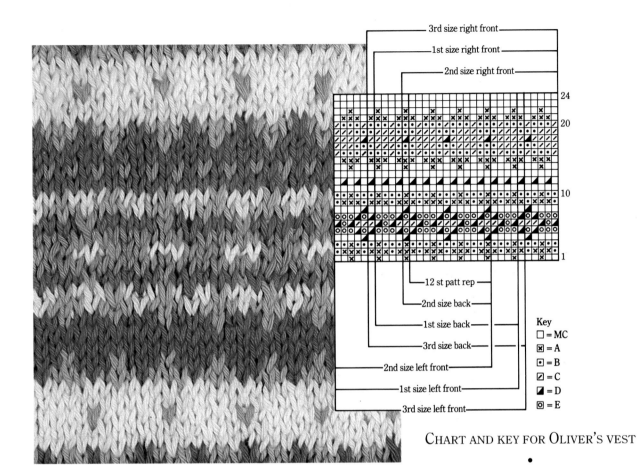

CHART AND KEY FOR OLIVER'S VEST

•

MATERIALS
Rowan Sea Breeze Soft Cotton 50g balls; Main color
(MC) Signal Red (532) or Turkish Plum (529) 2(2:3)
balls, contrasting color (A) Bleached (521) 1(1:1) ball.
1 pair each of 2mm (size 0) and 2³/₄mm (size 2) knitting
needles.
4(6:6) small buttons.

GAUGE
32 sts and 42 rows to 10cm (4in) square over st st on
2³/₄mm (size 2) needles.

BACK
With 2mm (size 0) needles and MC, cast on 70(84:92)
sts.
Work in K1 tbl, P1 rib for 4(5:5)cm [1¹/₂(2:2)in] inc to
76(92:100) sts in last row.
Change to 2³/₄mm (size 2) needles.
Beg K row, work in st st until back measures
15(20.5:23)cm [6(8:9)in], ending P row.

Shape armholes. Bind off 4 sts at beg of next 2 rows.
Dec one st each end of every row to 62(78:86) sts, then
every foll alt row to 60(72:80) sts.
Work straight until armholes measure 10(11.5:12.5)cm
[4(4¹/₂:5)in], ending P row.

Shape shoulders. Bind off 13(18:21) sts at beg of
next 2 rows.

Back neckband. Change to 2¹/₄mm (size 0) needles
and A. K 7 rows on rem 34(36:38) sts. Bind off.

FRONT
Work as given for back until front measures 10 rows
less than back to beg of shoulder shaping, ending P
row.

Shape neck. NEXT ROW K24(29:32), turn and leave
rem sts on a spare needle.
Bind off 3 sts at neck edge on next row, then 2 sts on
foll alt row. Dec one st at neck edge on every row to
13(18:21) sts, ending armhole edge.

BUTTONHOLE BAND
K 2 rows.
BUTTONHOLE ROW 1 K5(5:6), bind off 2, K next 0(4:5)
sts, bind off 0(2:2), K to end.
BUTTONHOLE ROW 2 K, casting on 2 sts over those bind
off. K 3 rows. Bind off.
With right side facing sl center 12(14:16) sts on a
holder, join yarn to rem sts and K to end. Work 1 row.
Complete to match first side.

ELIZABETH AND MILO IN THEIR EMBROIDERED PULLOVERS

•

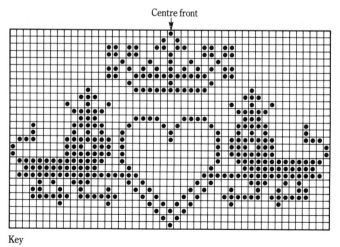

Centre front

Key
□ = MC
◉ = Swiss embroider in A

<u>S L E E V E S</u>
With 2mm (size 0) needles and MC, cast on 38(42:48) sts.
Work in K1 tbl, P1 rib for 4(5:5)cm [1½(2:2)in].
Change to 2¾mm (size 2) needles.
Beg K row, work in st st, inc one st each end of 5th and every foll 5th(4th:5th) row to 56(72:80) sts.
Work straight until sleeve measures 19(23:28)cm [7½(9:11)in], ending P row.

Shape sleeve top. Bind off 4 sts at beg of next 2 rows. Dec one st each end of every row to 40(54:62) sts, then on every foll alt row to 26(42:50) sts, then on every row to 22(24:24) sts. Bind off 3 sts at beg of next 4 rows. Bind off.

FRONT NECKBAND

With 2mm (size 0) needles, right side facing and A, pick up 15 sts down left front neck including row ends of buttonhole band, K front neck sts, pick up 15 sts up right front neck including row ends of buttonhole band. 42(44:46) sts.
K 2 rows.
BUTTONHOLE ROW 1 K3, bind off 2, K to last 5 sts, bind off 2, K3.
BUTTONHOLE ROW 2 K, casting on 2 sts over those bound off.
K 4 rows. Bind off.

TO MAKE UP

Duplicate stitch crest motif in A from chart center front of pullover, ending top of motif approx 4cm ($1^1/2$in) from top of neckband. Embroider chosen letters in heart as shown in the picture opposite. Lapping buttonhole bands over back shoulders, join row ends together at armhole edge. Set in sleeves. Join side and sleeve seams. Sew on buttons.

Laura's Pullover

Shown on page 98

MEASUREMENTS

To fit approx age 6 mths (2 yrs:4 yrs).
Actual chest measurement 48(58.5:63.5)cm [19(23:25)in].
Length 25.5(31.5:35.5)cm [10(12$^1/2$;14)in].
Sleeve seam 19(23:28)cm [7$^1/2$(9:11)in].

MATERIALS

Rowan Sea Breeze Soft Cotton 50g balls; 3(4:4) balls.
1 pair each of 2mm (size 0) and 2$^3/4$mm (size 2) knitting needles.
1 each of 2mm (size 0) and 2$^3/4$mm (size 2) set of 4 double-pointed knitting needles.
Approximately 540(580:620) pearls.

GAUGE

32 sts and 42 rows to 10cm (4in) square over st st on 2$^3/4$mm (size 2) needles.

SPECIAL ABBREVIATION

pearl 1 = slip pearl along yarn so pearl lies next to st just worked, then P1 to hold pearl in place.

Note Thread pearls onto yarn in manageable groups of approximately 40 pearls at a time, joining in and breaking off yarn as required.

BACK

With 2mm (size 0) needles and unbeaded yarn, cast on 70(84:92) sts.
Work in K1, P1 rib for 4(5:5)cm [1$^1/2$(2:2)in] inc to 76(92:100) sts in last row.

Change to 2$^3/4$mm (size 2) needles.
With beaded yarn, work in patt as follows:
ROW 1 (right side) K.
ROW 2 P.
ROW 3 K8(4:8), pearl 1, * K11, pearl 1; rep from * to last 7(3:7) sts, K7(3:7).
ROW 4 P.
ROWS 5 TO 10 Rep rows 1 and 2 three times.
ROW 11 K2(10:2), pearl 1, * K11, pearl 1; rep from * to last 1(9:1) sts, K1(9:1).
ROW 12 P.
ROWS 13 TO 16 Rep rows 1 and 2 twice.
These 16 rows form the patt.
Cont in patt until back measures 15(20.5:23)cm [6(8:9)in], ending wrong side row.

Shape armholes. Keeping patt correct, bind off 3(4:4) sts at beg of next 2 rows. Dec one st each end of every row to 60(72:80) sts.
Work straight until armholes measure 10(11.5:12.5)cm [4(4$^1/2$:5)in], ending wrong side row.

Shape shoulders. Bind off 6(9:10) sts at beg of next 2 rows, then 6(8:10) sts at beg of foll 2 rows. Leave rem sts on a holder.

FRONT

Work as given for back until front measures 12 rows **less** than back to beg of shoulder shaping, ending wrong side row.

Shape neck. NEXT ROW Patt 23(29:33), turn and leave rem sts on a spare needle.
Keeping patt correct, bind off 2(3:3) sts at neck edge on next row and 2(2:3) sts on foll alt row. Dec one st at neck edge on every row to 12(17:20) sts.
Work 1 row straight, ending armhole edge.

Shape shoulder. Bind off 6(9:10) sts at beg of next row. Work 1 row. Bind off.
With right side facing sl center 14 sts on a holder, join yarn to rem sts and patt to end. Work 1 row.
Complete to match first side.

SLEEVES

With 2mm (size 0) needles and unbeaded yarn, cast on 36(40:48) sts.
Work in K1, P1 rib for 4(5:5)cm [1$^1/2$(2:2)in].
Change to 2$^3/4$mm (size 2) needles.
With beaded yarn, work in patt as follows:
ROW 1 (right side) K.
ROW 2 P.
ROW 3 K12(2:6), pearl 1, * K11, pearl 1; rep from * to last 11(1:5) sts, K11(1:5).
Cont in patt as set, working as back, inc one st each end of foll 2nd and every foll 5th(3rd:4th) row to 52(48:52) sts, then on every foll 6th(4th:5th) row to 56(72:80) sts, working inc sts in patt.
Work straight until sleeve measures 19(23:28)cm [7$^1/2$(9:11)in], ending wrong side row.

LAURA TAKING REFUGE FROM THE SUN IN HER PEARL-TRIMMED SWEATER

•

Shape sleeve top. Keeping patt correct, bind off 3(4:4) sts at beg of next 2 rows. Dec one st each end of every row to 44(56:66) sts, then every foll alt row to 32(46:52) sts, then on every row to 22(26:28) sts. Bind off 3(3:4) sts at beg of next 2 rows, then 3(4:4) sts at beg of foll 2 rows. Bind off.

C O L L A R
Join shoulder seams. With 2mm (size 0) set of 4 needles, right side facing and unbeaded yarn, slip first 7 sts of center front neck on another holder, K rem 7 sts inc one st, pick up 17(18:19) sts up right front neck, K

back neck sts inc 5 sts, pick up 17(18:19) sts down left front neck, then inc one st and K rem front neck sts 91(95:99) sts. Turn. Work backwards and forwards in rows of rib as follows: Beg alt rows P1, work in K1, P1 rib for 2.5cm (1in). Change to $2^3/4$mm (size 2) set of 4 needles and cont in rib until collar measures 4(4.5:5)cm [$1^1/2(1^3/4:2)$in]. Bind off in rib.

T O   M A K E   U P
Set in sleeves. Join side and sleeve seams. At center front, catch-stitch together first two sts at base of collar to prevent neck from gaping.

Louisa's Sweater

Shown on page 101

MEASUREMENTS

To fit approx age 6 mths (2 yrs:4 yrs).
Actual chest measurement 48(58.5:63.5)cm
[19(23:25)in].
Length 30.5(37:40.5)cm (12(14½:16)in].
Sleeve seam 19(23:28)cm [7½(9:11)in].

MATERIALS

Rowan Handknit Cotton DK 50g balls; 7(7:8) balls.
1 pair each of 2¾mm (size 2) and 3¼mm (size 3)
knitting needles.
Cable needle.

GAUGE

30 sts and 34 rows to 10cm (4in) square over patt
(slightly stretched) on 3¼mm (size 3) needles.

SPECIAL ABBREVIATIONS

C4B = sl next 2 sts onto cable needle and leave at back
of work, K2, then K2 from cable needle.
C6B = sl next 3 sts onto cable needle and leave at back
of work, K3, then K3 from cable needle.
Note If binding off over a cable, [work 2 tog] 3 times,
while binding off in usual way.

BACK

With 2¾mm (size 2) needles cast on 47(52:63) sts.
P 1 row and K 1 row.
Now work in fancy rib as follows:
RIB ROW 1 (right side) K3(1:2), P1, K3, P1, * K4, P1,
K3, P1; rep from * to last 3(1:2) sts, K3(1:2).
RIB ROW 2 P3(1:2), K1, P3, K1, * P4, K1, P3, K1; rep
from * to last 3(1:2) sts, P3(1:2).
RIB ROW 3 K3(1:2), P5, * K4, P5; rep from * to last
3(1:2) sts, K3(1:2). **RIB ROW 4** As row 2.
RIB ROW 5 K3(1:2), P1, K3, P1, * C4B, P1, K3, P1; rep
from * to last 3(1:2) sts, K3(1:2).
RIB ROW 6 P3(1:2), K5, * P4, K5; rep from * to last
3(1:2) sts, P3(1:2).
Cont in fancy rib until waistband measures 4(5:5)cm
[1½(2:2)in], ending wrong side row and inc to 72(86:94)
sts in last row.
Change to 3¼mm (size 3) needles.
Work in patt as follows:
ROW 1 (right side) P0(0:3), K0(0:1), P0(3:3), K0(1:1),
P0(3:3), K3, P3, K1, P3, * K6, P3, K1, P3, K3, P3,
K1, P3; rep from * to last 16(0:4) sts, K6(0:0),
P3(0:0), K1(0:1), P3(0:3), K3(0:0).
ROW 2 K0(0:3), P0(0:1), K0(3:3), P0(1:1), K0(3:3),
P3, K3, P1, K3, * P6, K3, P1, K3, P3, K3, P1, K3; rep
from * to last 16(0:4) sts, P6(0:0), K3(0:0), P1(0:1),
K3(0:3), P3(0:0).
ROW 3 As row 1.
ROW 4 K10(17:21), * P6, K17; rep from * to last
16(0:4) sts, P6(0:0), K10(0:4).
ROW 5 P0(0:3), K0(0:1), P0(3:3), K0(1:1), P0(3:3),

K3, P3, K1, P3, * C6B, P3, K1, P3, K3, P3, K1, P3;
rep from * to last 16(0:4) sts, C6B(0:0), P3(0:0),
K1(0:1), P3(0:3), K3(0:0).
ROW 6 As row 2.
ROWS 7 AND 8 As rows 1 and 4.
These 8 rows form the patt.
Cont in patt until back measures 20.5(25.5:28)cm
[8(10:11)in], ending wrong side row.

Shape armholes. Keeping patt correct, bind off
6(8:9) sts at beg of next 2 rows. 60(70:76) sts.
Work straight until armholes measure 10(11.5:12.5)cm
[4(4½:5)in], ending wrong side row.
NEXT ROW Bind off 14(18:20) sts, patt to last 14(18:20)
sts and bind off these sts. Leave rem sts on a holder.

FRONT

Work as given for back until armholes measure
5.5(6.5:7)cm [2¼(2½:2¾)in], ending wrong side row.

Shape neck. NEXT ROW Patt 23(27:29), turn and leave
rem sts on a spare needle.
Keeping patt correct bind off 2 sts at neck edge on next
and foll alt row. Dec one st at neck edge on every foll alt
row to 14(18:20) sts.
Work a few rows straight until armhole measures same
as back to shoulder, ending wrong side row. Bind off.
With right side facing, sl center 14(16:18) sts on a
holder, join yarn to rem sts and patt to end.
Work 1 row. Complete to match first side.

SLEEVES

With 2¾mm (size 2) needles cast on 28(28:30) sts.
P 1 row and K 1 row.
Now work in fancy rib as follows:
RIB ROW 1 (right side) K2(2:3), P1, * K4, P1, K3, P1;
rep from * to last 7(7:8) sts, K4, P1, K2(2:3).
RIB ROW 2 P2(2:3), K1, * P4, K1, P3, K1; rep from * to
last 7(7:8) sts, P4, P1, P2(2:3).
Cont in fancy rib as set, working as back, for 4(5:5)cm
[1½(2:2)in], ending wrong side row and inc to 37(37:45)
sts in last row.
Change to 3¼mm (size 3) needles.
Work in patt as follows:
ROW 1 (right side) K0(0:1), P0(0:3), K1, P3, K6, P3,
K1, P3, K3, P3, K1, P3, K6, P3, K1, P0(0:3), K0(0:1).
ROW 2 P0(0:1), K0(0:3), P1, K3, P6, K3, P1, K3, P3,
K3, P1, K3, P6, K3, P1, K0(0:3), P0(0:1).
Cont in patt as set, working as back, inc one st each end
of next, then every foll 4th(3rd:4th) row to 55(55:59)
sts, then on every foll 5th(4th:5th) row to 59(67:75)
sts, working sts into patt.
Work straight until sleeve measures 19(23:28)cm
[7½(9:11)in], ending wrong side row.
Place a marker each end of last row.
Work another 6(8:10) rows. Bind off.

NECKBAND

Join right shoulder seam.
With 2¾mm (size 2) needles and right side facing, pick

up 12(13:13) sts down left front neck, K front neck sts, pick up 12(13:13) sts up right front neck, then K back neck sts dec 5(7:5) sts. 65(69:75) sts.
Work in fancy rib as follows:
RIB ROW 1 (wrong side) K0(1:0), P3(4:1), * K1, P3, K1, P4; rep from * to last 8(1:2) sts, K1, P3(0:1), K1(0:0), P3(0:0).
Cont in fancy rib as set for 5.5(6.5:7.5)cm [2¼(2½:3)in].
With 3¼mm (size 3) needles, bind off loosely in rib.

TO MAKE UP

Join left shoulder and neckband seam. Turn neckband in half to wrong side and sew in place. Set in sleeves, sewing row ends above markers to bound-off sts at underarms. Join side and sleeve seams.

Jamie's Cardigan

MEASUREMENTS

To fit approx age 6 mths (2 yrs:4 yrs).
Actual chest measurement 48(58.5:63.5)cm [19(23:25)in].
Length 25.5(31.5:35.5)cm [10(12½:14)in].
Sleeve seam 19(23:28)cm [7½(9:11)in].

MATERIALS

Rowan Handknit Cotton DK 50g balls; 5(6:7) balls.
1 pair each of 2¾mm (size 2) and 3¼mm (size 3) knitting needles.
4 buttons.

GAUGE

24 sts and 32 rows to 10cm (4in) square over st st on 3¼mm (size 3) needles.

Note To help ribbed edges to keep their elasticity, shirring elastic can be knitted in with the cotton yarn.

BACK

With 2¾mm (size 2) needles cast on 50(62:68) sts.
Work in K, P, rib for 4(5:5)cm [1½(2:2)in] inc to 57(69:75) sts in last row.
Change to 3¼mm (size 3) needles.
Beg K row, work in st st until back measures 15(20.5:23)cm [6(8:9)in], ending P row.

Shape armholes. Bind off 2(3:3) sts at beg of next 2 rows. Dec one st each end of every row to 45(53:59) sts.
Work straight until armholes measure 10(11.5:12.5)cm [4(4½:5)in], ending P row.

Shape shoulders. Bind off 5(7:8) sts at beg of next 2 rows, then 5(6:7) sts at beg of foll 2 rows. Bind off rem sts.

LEFT FRONT

With 2¾mm (size 2) needles cast on 38(44:48) sts.
Work in K1, P1 rib for 4(5:5)cm [1½(2:2)in] inc 3(4:4) sts over last 13(17:19) sts (for right front read first 13[17:19] sts here) on last row. 41(48:52) sts.
Change to 3¼mm (size 3) needles
ROW 1 (right side) K.
ROW 2 K25(27:29), P16(21:23).
Rep last 2 rows until front measures same as back to beg of armhole shaping, ending wrong side row (for right front end right side row here).

Shape armhole. Keeping front garter st border correct, bind off 2(3:3) sts at beg of next row.
Work 1 row (for right front omit this row).
Dec one st at armhole edge on every row to 35(40:44) sts.
Work straight until armhole measures same as back to beg of shoulder shaping, ending armhole edge.

Shape shoulder. Bind off 5(7:8) sts at beg of next row, then 5(6:7) sts at beg of foll alt row. 25(27:29) sts.
Cont straight on rem sts until garter st border fits across to center back neck, ending right side row (for right front end wrong side row here).

Shape border. NEXT 2 ROWS K21(23:25), turn, sl 1, K to end.
NEXT 2 ROWS K17(19:21), turn, sl 1, K to end.
NEXT 2 ROWS K13(15:17), turn, sl 1, K to end.

LOUISA'S CRUNCHY-TEXTURED COTTON
PULLOVER IS IDEAL FOR A WARM SPRING DAY

Cont in this way until the rows K5(3:5), turn, sl 1, K to end have been worked. Bind off.

RIGHT FRONT

Work as given for left front, noting exceptions in parentheses, reversing garter st front border and making buttonholes when front measures approx 2.5cm (1in) and 7.5(9:10)cm [3(3½:4)in] from beg as follows:
BUTTONHOLE ROW 1 (right side) Patt 5, bind off 3, patt next 8(10:12) sts, bind off 3, patt to end.
BUTTONHOLE ROW 2 Patt, casting on 3 sts over those bound off.

SLEEVES

With 2¾mm (size 2) needles, cast on 28(30:36) sts.
Work in K1, P1 rib for 4(5:5)cm [1½(2:2)in].
Change to 3¼mm (size 3) needles.
Beg K row and working in st st, inc one st each end of 3rd, then every foll 5th(4th:5th) row to 32(50:50) sts, then on every foll 6th(5th:6th) row to 42(54:60) sts.
Work straight until sleeve measures 19(23:28)cm [7½(9:11)in], ending P row.

Shape top. Bind off 2(3:3) sts at beg of next 2 rows.
Dec one st each end of every row to 32(42:48) sts, then every foll alt row to 28(38:40) sts, then on every row to 14(16:18) sts. Bind off 2 sts at beg of next 2 rows, then 2(3:3) sts at beg of foll 2 rows. Bind off.

TO MAKE UP

Join shoulder seams. Join bound-off edges of garter st border together, then sew row ends of border to back neck. Set in sleeves. Join side and sleeve seams. Sew on buttons.

Ashley's Pullover

MEASUREMENTS

To fit approx age 6 mths (2 yrs:4 yrs).
Actual chest measurement 48(58.5:63.5)cm [19(23:25)in].
Length 25.5(31.5:35.5)cm [10(12½:14)in].
Sleeve seam 19(23:28)cm [7½(9:11)in].

MATERIALS

Rowan Sea Breeze Soft Cotton 50g balls: 4(4:5) balls.
1 pair each of 2mm (size 0) and 2¾mm (size 2) knitting needles.
crochet hook.
2 buttons.

GAUGE

30 sts and 40 rows to 10cm (4in) square over patt on 2¾mm (size 2) needles.

SPECIAL ABBREVIATION

MB = [K into front, back, front, back and front] of next

st, turn, P5, turn, K5, turn, P5, turn, sl 1, K1, psso, sl 1, k2 tog, pass 2nd and 3rd sts over first st.

BACK

With 2mm (size 0) needles cast on 62(78:82) sts.
Beg alt rows P2, work in K2, P2 rib for 4(5:5)cm [1½(2:2)in], ending wrong side row and inc to 71(87:95) sts in last row.
Change to 2¾mm (size 2) needles.
Beg K row, work 4 rows in st st.
Work in patt as follows:
ROW 1 (right side) K11(7:11), MB, * K11, MB; rep from * to last 11(7:11) sts, K to end.
ROW 2 P.
ROW 3 K.
ROW 4 P.
ROW 5 K9(5:9), MB, K3, MB, * K7, MB, K3, MB; rep from * to last 9(5:9) sts, K to end.
ROWS 6 TO 8 As rows 2 to 4.
ROW 9 K7(3:7), MB, K7, MB, * K3, MB, K7, MB; rep from * to last 7(3:7) sts, K to end.
ROWS 10 TO 12 As rows 2 to 4.
ROW 13 K5(1:5), MB, * K11, MB; rep from * to last 5(1:5) sts, K to end.
ROWS 14 TO 24 Reverse patt by working row 12 back to row 2 in this order.
These 24 rows form the patt.
Cont in patt until back measures 25.5(31.5:35.5)cm [10(12½:14)in], ending wrong side row.

Shape shoulders. Keeping patt correct, bind off 7(9:11) sts at beg of next 2 rows, 7(9:10) sts at beg of foll 2 rows, then 6(8:9) sts at beg of next 2 rows.
Leave rem sts on a holder.

FRONT

Work as given for back until front measures 8(8:10) rows **less** than back to beg of shoulder shaping, ending wrong side row.

Shape neck. NEXT ROW Patt 29(36:40), turn and leave rem sts on a spare needle.
Keeping patt correct, bind off 3 sts at neck edge on next row, then 2(3:3) sts on foll alt row. Dec one st at neck edge on every row to 20(26:30) sts.
Work 0(0:2) rows straight, ending side edge.

Shape shoulder. Bind off 7(9:11) sts at beg of next row, then 7(9:10) sts on foll alt row. Work 1 row. Bind off.
With right side facing sl center 13(15:15) sts on a holder, join yarn to rem sts and patt to end.
Work 1 row. Complete to match first side.

SLEEVES

With 2mm (size 0) needles cast on 34(38:46) sts.
Beg alt rows P2, work in K2, P2 rib for 4(5:5)cm [1½(2:2)in], ending wrong side row and inc to 35(41:47) sts in last row.

ASHLEY'S BOBBLE KNIT WORKED IN A SOFT GRAY COTTON YARN

•

Change to 2³/₄mm (size 2) needles.
Beg K row, work 4 rows in st st, inc one st each end of
4th row. 37(43:49) sts.
Work in patt as follows:
ROW 1 (right side) K6(9:12), MB, * K11, MB; rep from
* to last 6(9:12) sts, K to end.
ROW 2 P.
ROW 3 K.
ROW 4 P, but inc one st each end of row on **1st and
2nd sizes only**.
ROW 5 K0(0:2), 0(0:MB), K5(8:7), MB, K3, MB, * K7,
MB, K3, MB; rep from * to last 5(8:10) sts, K5(8:7),
0(0:MB), K0(0:2).
Cont in patt as set, working as back and inc one st each
end of every 5th(5th:6th) row from last inc to 57(55:75)
sts, then on **2nd size only** on every 4th row to 69 sts,
working inc sts in patt on **all sizes**.
Cont straight until sleeve measures 19(23:28) cm
[7¹/₂(9:11)in], ending wrong side row. Bind off.

NECKBAND
Join right shoulder seam.
With 2mm (size 0) needles and right side facing, pick up
13(13:14) sts down left front neck, K front neck sts inc
1(0:1) st, pick up 13(13:14) sts up right front neck, then
K back neck sts inc 3(2:3) sts. 74 (78:82) sts.
Beg alt rows P2, work in K2, P2 rib for 1.5cm (¹/₂in).
With 2³/₄mm (size 2) needles, bind off in rib.

TO MAKE UP
Join left shoulder seam for 3(5:5.5)cm [1¹/₄(2:2¹/₄)in]
leaving remainder of shoulder and neckband open. Sew
on sleeves, placing center of bound-off edges of sleeves
at shoulder seams. Join side and sleeve seams. Crochet
a row of slip stitch round shoulder opening, then
another row of slip stitch along front edge only working
2 button loops. Sew buttons on back edge to match.

Edward's Vest

MEASUREMENTS
To fit approx age 2 yrs (4 yrs).
Actual chest measurement 56(61)cm [22(24)in].
Length 29(33)cm [11¹⁄₂(13)in] from top of shoulder to
bottom of back.

MATERIALS
Rowan Handknit Cotton DK 50g balls; Main color (MC)
Bleached (263) 4(5:5) balls, contrasting color (A)
Turkish Plum (277) 1(2:3) balls.
1 pair each of 2³⁄₄mm (size 2) and 3¹⁄₄mm (size 3)
knitting needles.
5 buttons.

GAUGE
26 sts and 28 rows to 10cm (4in) square over patt on
3¹⁄₄mm (size 3) needles.

SPECIAL ABBREVIATIONS
pw = purlwise.
kw = knitwise.

Note When working patt from chart strand yarn not in
use loosely across back of work over no more than 3 sts
at a time, making sure that the same gauge is obtained
throughout.

BACK
With 2³⁄₄mm (size 2) needles and MC, cast on 71(77)
sts.
SEED ST ROW K1, [P1, K1] to end.
Rep this row for 1.5cm (¹⁄₂in).
Change to 3¹⁄₄mm (size 3) needles.
Cont in seed st until waistband measures 2cm (³⁄₄in).
Beg K row, work in st st from chart following markers
for back until back measures approx 18(20.5)cm
[7(8)in], ending patt row 14(20).

Shape armholes. Keeping patt correct, bind off 3 sts
at beg of next 2 rows. Dec one st each of every row to
53(59) sts.
Work straight until armholes measure 11.5(12.5)cm
[4¹⁄₂(5)in], ending P row.

Shape shoulders. Bind off 6(7) sts at beg of next 4
rows. Bind off rem sts.

LEFT FRONT
With 3¹⁄₄mm (size 3) needles and MC, cast on 2 sts.
NEXT ROW (right side) K 1MC, 1A. **NEXT ROW** With MC
inc pw in first st, P 1MC. **NEXT ROW** With MC bind on
7(8) sts and work as follows: K 4(5)MC, 1A, 3MC, 1A,
with MC inc kw in last st.

•

THE FRONT VIEW OF OLIVER'S PULLOVER IS LIKE
ANTONIA'S (PAGE 79). AT RIGHT, EDWARD'S VEST

NEXT ROW With MC inc pw in first st, P 4MC, 1A,
1MC, 1A, 3(4)MC.
NEXT ROW With MC cast on 7 sts and work as follows:
K 0(1)A, 3MC, 1A, 7MC, 1A, 3MC, 1A, 2MC, with
MC inc kw in last st.
NEXT ROW With MC inc pw in first st, P 1A, [5MC, 1A,
1MC, 1A] twice, 2(3)MC.
NEXT ROW With MC cast on 7 sts and work as follows:
K 0(1)MC, [1A, 1MC] 14 times.
NEXT ROW P [1A, 1MC] 14 times, 0(1)A.
NEXT ROW With MC cast on 5(7) sts and work as
follows: K 0(2)MC, 0(1)A, 7MC, [1A, 3MC] twice, 1A,
7MC, [1A, 3MC] twice, 1A, 1MC. 33(36) sts.
The last row was row 1 of chart.
Cont in patt as set, working in st st from chart,
following markers for left front until straight edge of left
front side seam measures same as back to beg of
armhole shaping (omitting seed st waistband), ending
patt row 14(20) (for right front end patt row 15(21)
here).

Shape armhole and front neck. Keeping patt
correct, bind off 3 sts at beg of next row.
Work 1 row (omit this row when working right front).
Dec one st at front edge on next and every foll alt row,
at the same time, dec one st at armhole edge on
every row to 21(24) sts.
Keeping armhole edge straight, cont to dec at front
edge on every foll alt row from last dec to 16(18) sts,
then on every foll 3rd row to 12(14) sts.
Work a few rows straight until front measures same as
back to beg of shoulder shaping, ending armhole edge.

Shape shoulder. Bind off 6(7) sts at beg of next row.
Work 1 row. Bind off.

RIGHT FRONT
With 3¹⁄₄mm (size 3) needles and MC, cast on 2 sts.
NEXT ROW (right side) K 1A, 1MC.
NEXT ROW P 1MC, with MC inc pw in last st.
NEXT ROW With MC inc kw in first st, 1A, 1MC.
NEXT ROW With MC cast on 7(8) sts and work as
follows: P 3(4)MC, 1A, 1MC, 1A, 4MC, with MC inc
pw in last st.
NEXT ROW With MC inc kw in first st, K 2MC, 1A,
3MC, 1A, 4(5)MC.
NEXT ROW With MC cast on 7 sts and work as follows: P
2(3)MC, [1A, 1MC, 1A, 5MC] twice, 1A, with MC inc
pw in last st.
NEXT ROW K [1MC, 1A] 10(11) times, 1(0)MC.
NEXT ROW With MC cast on 7 sts and work as follows: P
0(1)A, [1MC, 1A] 14 times.
NEXT ROW K 1MC, 1A, 3MC, 1A, 3MC, 1A, 7MC, 1A,
3MC, 1A, 3MC, 1A, 2(3)MC.
NEXT ROW With MC cast on 5(7) sts and work as
follows: P 0(1)MC, 0(1)A, 0(1)MC, 1A, [5MC, 1A,
1MC, 1A] 4 times. 33(36) sts.
The last row was row 2 of chart.
Cont as given for left front, working in st st from chart
following markers for right front and noting exceptions
in parentheses.

Chart 1

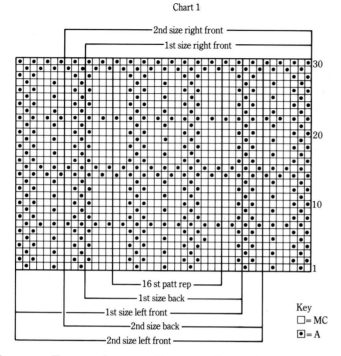

Chart 2

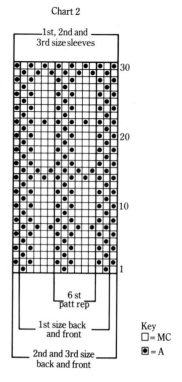

CHART 1: EDWARD'S VEST. CHART 2: OLIVER'S PULLOVER

•

FRONT BOTTOM EDGING AND BUTTON
BAND

With 2³/₄mm (size 2) needles and MC cast on 6 sts.
ROW 1 (right side) [K1, P1] to end.
ROW 2 [P1, K1] to end.
Rep these 2 rows for seed st patt.
Cont in patt until band, slightly stretched, measures
from side seam of front to inner edge of point, ending
outer edge.
Work mitered corner as follows:
*NEXT 2 ROWS Patt 2, turn, sl 1, patt 1.
NEXT 2 ROWS Patt 3, turn, sl 1, patt to end.
NEXT 2 ROWS Patt 4, turn, sl 1, patt to end.
NEXT 2 ROWS Patt 5, turn, sl 1, patt to end*.
Work straight across all sts until band, slightly
stretched, measures from point to beg of straight front
edge, ending outer edge.
Rep from * to * for 2nd mitered corner.
Work straight across all sts until band, slightly
stretched, fits up front edge to beg of neck shaping,
ending at inner edge.

Shape lapel. Inc one st at inner edge on next and
every foll alt row to 11(13) sts, working inc sts in patt.
Work straight until lapel measures 7.5(8)cm [3(3¹/₄)in]
from beg of incs, ending at straight edge.
Bind off in patt. Sew edging and band in place.
Place markers on band for 5 buttons, first at top of 2nd
mitered corner, last at beg of lapel (neck) shaping and
rem evenly spaced between.

FRONT BOTTOM EDGING AND
BUTTONHOLE BAND

Work as given for front bottom edging and button band
reversing shaping and making buttonholes to match
markers as follows:
BUTTONHOLE ROW 1 (right side) Patt 2, bind off 2, patt
to end.
BUTTONHOLE ROW 2 Patt, casting on 2 sts over those
bound off.

COLLAR

With 2³/₄mm (size 2) needles and MC cast on 23(25) sts.
Working in seed st as given for back waistband and
keeping patt correct, bind on 4(5) sts at beg of next 4
rows, then 5 sts at beg of foll 2 rows, working inc sts in
patt. 49(55) sts.
Cont straight in patt until straight edge of row ends
measure 5(5.5)cm [2(2¹/₄)in]. Bind off loosely in patt.

ARMHOLE BANDS

Join shoulder seams.
With 2³/₄mm (size 2) needles, right side facing and MC,
pick up 79(87) sts around armhole edge.
Work in seed st as given for back waistband for 1.5cm
(¹/₂in), dec one st each end of every row. Bind off in
patt.

TO MAKE UP

Sew cast-on edge of collar to back neck, starting and
ending at top of front bands, then join bound-off edge of
front bands to row ends of collar for 2(2.5)cm [³/₄(1)in]
from inner edge, leaving remainder of seam free. Join
side and armhole band seams, matching front bands to
back waistband. Sew on buttons.

Antonia's Pullover

MEASUREMENTS
To fit approx age 6 mths (2 yrs:4 yrs).
Actual chest measurement (unstretched)
45(54:59.5)cm[17³/₄(21¹/₄:23¹/₂)in].
Length 30.5(37:40.5) [12(14¹/₂:16)in].
Sleeve seam approx 19(23:28)cm [7¹/₂(9:11)in].

MATERIALS
Rowan Handknit Cotton DK 50g balls; Main color (MC)
Bleached (263) 6(7:7) balls, 1st contrasting color (A)
China (267) 1(1:1) ball, 2nd contrasting color (B) Purple
(272) 1(1:1) ball.
1 pair each of 2³/₄mm (size 2) and 3¹/₄mm (size 3)
knitting needles.
Cable needle.

GAUGE
27 sts and 32 rows to 10cm (4in) square over patt
(unstretched) on 3¹/₄mm (size 3) needles.

SPECIAL ABBREVIATION
C6F = sl next 3 sts onto cable needle and leave at front
of work, K3, then K3 from cable needle.

Note If binding off over a cable, [work 2 tog] 3 times,
while binding off in usual way.

BACK
With 2³/₄mm (size 2) needles and MC, cast on 50(62:68)
sts.
Work in K1, P1 rib for 4 rows.
Change to A, K 1 row, then rib 1 row, change to MC, K
1 row, then rib 1 row, change to B, K 1 row, then rib 1
row, change to MC, K 1 row, then cont in MC only until
rib measures 4(5:5)cm [1¹/₂(2:2)in] inc to 60(73:82) sts
in last row.
Change to 3¹/₄mm (size 3) needles.
ROW 1 (right side) P2(3:2), K1, P2, * K6, P2, K1, P2;
rep from * to last 0(1:0) st, P0(1:0).
ROW 2 K5(6:5), * P6, K5; rep from * to last 0(1:0) st,
K0(1:0).
ROW 3 P2(3:2), K1, P2, * C6F, P2, K1, P2; rep from *
to last 0(1:0) st, P0(1:0).
ROW 4 As row 2. **ROWS 5 AND 6** As rows 1 and 2.
These 6 rows form the patt.
Cont in patt until back measures 20.5(25.5:28)cm
[8(10:11)in], ending wrong side row.

Shape armholes. Keeping patt correct, bind off
2(3:4) sts at beg of next 2 rows. Dec one st each end of
next 3(3:4) rows. 50(61:66) sts.
Work straight until armholes measure 10(11.5:12.5)cm
[4(4¹/₂:5)in], ending wrong side row.

Shape shoulders. Bind off 5(8:9) sts at beg of next 2
rows, then 5(7:8) sts at beg of foll 2 rows. Leave rem
sts on a holder.

Work as given for back until front measures 2 rows
less than back to beg of armhole shaping, ending wrong
side row.

Shape neck. NEXT ROW Patt 30(36:41), turn and leave
rem sts on a spare needle.
Keeping patt correct, dec one st at neck edge on next
row. 29(35:40) sts.

Shape armhole. Bind off 2(3:4) sts at beg of next
row. Dec one st at neck edge on every alt row from last
dec, AT THE SAME TIME, dec one st at armhole
edge on 2nd and foll 2(2:3) rows. 22(27:29) sts.
Keeping armhole edge straight, cont to dec at neck
edge on every foll alt row from last dec to 10(19:21)
sts, then on **2nd and 3rd sizes only**, dec one st at
neck edge on every foll 3rd row to (15:17) sts.
On all sizes, work a few rows straight until front
measures same as back to beg of shoulder shaping,
ending armhole edge.

Shape shoulder. Bind off 5(8:9) sts at beg of next
row. Work 1 row. Bind off.
With right side facing, sl center 0(1:0) st on a holder,
join yarn to rem sts and patt to end. Dec one st at neck
edge on next row. Work 1 row.

Shape armhole. Bind off 2(3:4) sts, patt to last 2 sts,
work 2 tog.
Dec one st at neck edge on every alt row from last dec,

AT THE SAME TIME, dec one st at armhole edge on next 3(3:4) rows. 22(27:29) sts.
Complete to match first side.

SLEEVES

With 2³/₄mm (size 2) needles and MC, cast on 28(30:36) sts.
Work in K1, P1 rib in MC only until rib measures 4(5:5)cm [1¹/₂(2:2)in] inc to 32(32:38) sts in last row.
Change to 3¹/₄mm (size 3) needles.
ROW 1 (right side) P0(0:2), K0(0:1), P2, * K6, P2, K1, P2; rep from * to last 8(8:0) sts, K6(6:0), P2(2:0).
ROW 2 K2(2:5), * P6, K5; rep from * to last 8(8:0) sts, P6(6:0), K2(2:0).
Cont in patt as set, inc one st each end of next and every foll 6th(3rd:4th) row to 42(42:50) sts, then on every foll 6th(4th:5th) row to 46(58:66) sts, working inc sts in patt.
Work straight until sleeve measures approx 19(23:28)cm [7¹/₂(9:11)in], ending wrong side row and same cable patt row as back to beg of armhole shaping.

Shape top. Bind off 2(3:4) sts at beg of next 2 rows.
Dec one st each end of every row to 36(46:54) sts, then every foll alt row to 32(44:50) sts, then on every row to 18(18:20) sts. Bind off 2 sts at beg of next 2 rows, then 3 sts at beg of foll 2 rows. Bind off.

NECKBAND

Join right shoulder seam.
With 2³/₄mm (size 2) needles and right side facing and MC, pick up 31(33:37) sts down left front neck, pick up one st at center front on **1st and 3rd sizes**, K center front neck st on **2nd size**, mark this st, pick up 30(32:36) sts up right front neck, then K back neck sts, dec 3 sts across each group of cables. 83(91:97) sts.
RIB ROW (wrong side) K1, * P1, K1; rep from * to end.
This row sets the rib.
Change to A, K 1 row, then rib 1 row, change to B, K 1 row, then rib 1 row, change to MC, K 1 row, then rib 1 row, AT THE SAME TIME, dec one st either side of center marked st on every row.
With MC, bind off in rib, dec as before.

TO MAKE UP

Join left shoulder and neckband seam. Set in sleeves.
Join side and sleeve seams.

Oliver's Pullover

Shown on page 104, left

MEASUREMENTS

To fit approx age 6 mths (2 yrs:4 yrs).
Actual chest measurement 48(58.5:63.5)cm [19(23:25)in].
Length 25.5(31.5:35.5)cm [10(12¹/₂:14)in].
Sleeve seam 19(23:28)cm [7¹/₂(9:11)in].

MATERIALS

Rowan Handknit Cotton DK 50g balls; Main color (MC) Turkish Plum (277) 4(5:5) balls, contrasting color (A) Bleached (263) 2(3:3) balls.
1 pair each of 2³/₄mm (size 2) and 3¹/₄mm (size 3) knitting needles.
1 each of 2³/₄mm (size 2) and 3¹/₄mm (size 3) set of 4 double-pointed knitting needles.

GAUGE

26 sts and 28 rows to 10cm (4in) square over patt on 3¹/₄mm (size 3) needles.

Note When working patt from chart strand yarn not in use loosely across back of work over no more than 3 sts at a time, making sure that the same gauge is obtained throughout.

BACK

With 2³/₄mm (size 2) needles and MC, cast on 50(62:68) sts.
Work in K1, P1 rib for 4(5:5)cm [1¹/₂(2:2)in] inc to

EDWARD'S SLEEVELESS PULLOVER – ALL READY FOR GAME, SET, AND MATCH!

61(75:81) sts in last row.
Change to 3¼mm (size 3) needles.
Beg K row, work in st st from chart 2 (page 106) following markers for back until back measures approx 15(20.5:23)cm [6(8:9)in], ending patt row 2(12:20).

Shape armholes. Bind off 2(3:3) sts at beg of next 2 rows.
Dec one st each end of every row to 49(59:65) sts.
Work straight until armholes measure 10(11.5:12.5)cm [4(4½:5)in], ending P row.

Shape shoulders. Keeping patt correct, bind off 5(7:8) sts at beg of next 4 rows. Leave rem sts on a holder.

FRONT

Work as given for back, following markers for front, until front is 8(8:10) rows **less** than back to beg of shoulder shaping, ending P row.

Shape neck. NEXT ROW Patt 19(23:26), turn and leave rem sts on a spare needle.
Keeping patt correct, bind off 3 sts at neck edge on next row, then 2 sts at beg of foll alt row. Dec one st at neck edge on every row to 10(14:16) sts.
Work 0(0:1) row straight, ending armhole edge.

Shape shoulder. Bind off 5(7:8) sts at beg of next row. Work 1 row. Bind off.
With right side facing sl center 11(13:13) sts on a holder, join yarn to rem sts and patt to end. Work 1 row. Complete to match first side.

SLEEVES

With 2¾mm (size 2) needles and MC, cast on 28(30:36) sts.
Work in K1, P1 rib for 4(5:5)cm [1½(2:2)in] inc to 33(33:39) sts in last row.
Change to 3¼mm (size 3) needles.
Beg K row and patt row 21(23:17), work in st st from chart following markers for sleeves, inc one st each end of 5th, then every foll 6th(3rd:4th) row to 41(55:61) sts, then every foll 7th(4th:5th) row to 45(59:65) sts, working inc sts in patt.
Work straight until sleeve measures approx 19(23:28)cm [7½(9:11)in], ending patt row 2(12:20).

Shape top. Keeping patt correct, bind off 2(3:3) sts at beg of next 2 rows. Dec one st each end of every row to 35(47:53) sts, then every foll alt row to 31(45:49) sts, then every row to 21(23:27) sts. Bind off 3(3:4) sts at beg of next 4 rows. Bind off.

COLLAR

Join shoulder seams.
With 2¾mm (size 2) set of 4 needles, right side facing and MC, sl first 5(6:6) sts of center front neck onto another holder, K rem front neck sts from holder, pick up 14(14:16) sts up right front neck, K back neck sts

inc 4 sts, pick up 14(14:16) sts down left front neck inc one st, then K front neck sts from holder. 73(77:83) sts. Turn.
Work backwards and forwards in rows of rib as follows:
Beg alt rows P1, work in K1, P1 rib for 2.5cm (1in).
Change to 3¼mm (size 3) set of 4 needles and cont in rib as set until collar measures 5(5.5:6.5)cm [2(2¼:2½)in]. Bind off loosely in rib.

TO MAKE UP

Set in sleeves. Join side and sleeve seams. At center front, catch-stitch together first two sts at base of collar to prevent neck from gaping.

•

Edward's Pullover

MEASUREMENTS

To fit approx age 6 mths (2 yrs:4 yrs).
Actual chest measurement (unstretched) 45(54:59.5)cm[17¾(21¼:23½)in].
Length 30.5(37:40.5)cm [12(14½:16)in].

MATERIALS

Rowan Handknit Cotton DK 50g balls; Main color (MC) Bleached (263) 3(4:4) balls, 1st contrasting color (A) Clover (266) 1(1:1) ball, 2nd contrasting color (B) Yellow (271) 1(1:1) ball.
1 pair each of 2¾mm (size 2) and 3¼mm (size 3) knitting needles.
Cable needle.

GAUGE

27 sts and 32 rows to 10cm (4in) square over patt (unstretched) on 3¼mm (size 3) needles.

SPECIAL ABBREVIATION

C6F = sl next 3 sts onto cable needle and leave at front of work, K3, then K3 from cable needle.

Note If binding off over a cable, [work 2 tog] 3 times, while binding off in usual way.

BACK, FRONT AND NECKBAND

Work as given for back, front and neckband of Julian's pullover (page 17).

ARMHOLE BANDS

Join left shoulder and neckband seam.
With 2¾mm (size 2) needles and MC, pick 70(78:86) sts around armhole edge.
Work in K1, P1 rib in MC for 1.5cm (½in), dec one st each end of every row. Bind off in rib.

TO MAKE UP

Join side and armhole band seams.

Techniques of knitting

KNITTING WITH MORE THAN ONE COLOR

There are three basic methods of working with more than one color in a row.

Weaving. This is used when contrasting yarn must be carried behind the main color for more than four stitches. (Figs 1–5)

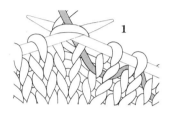

Fig 1 On a K row, hold the contrasting yarn at the back of work in the left hand.

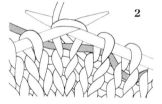

Fig 2 As you knit the stitch, bring the contrasting yarn below the main color yarn. When the contrasting yarn is being knitted, weave the main color in the same way.

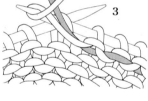

Fig 3 On a P row, hold the contrasting yarn at the front of work in the left hand.

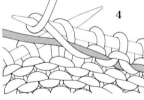

Fig 4 As the stitch is purled, bring the contrasting yarn below the main color.

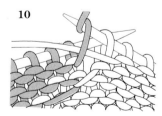

Fig 5 If weaving has been correctly worked the yarns will cross evenly.

Stranding. This method can be used to carry contrasting yarn up to four stitches behind the main color, but no more than this, as the elasticity of the knitting would be lost. This method is usually used when knitting Fair Isle patterns. (Figs 6–8).

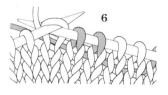

Fig 6 With both yarns at back of work, knit the specified stitches in the main color, then drop yarn at back. Pick up contrasting yarn, knit, then drop at back.

Fig 7 On a P row, hold both yarns at front, purl specified stitches in main color, then drop the yarns. Pick up contrasting yarn, purl, then drop. Both yarns stranded along side facing you.

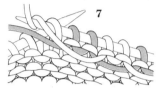

Fig 8 If stranding has been correctly worked, yarns will be running evenly across without puckering.

Crossing yarn in block colors (intarsia). In certain designs, blocks of separate colors are used. You will find it easier to work if you wind a small amount of each color onto a bobbin. Yarns are then less likely to tangle. At each color change, yarn should be twisted with the color next to it to prevent a hole from forming in the knitting. (Figs 9 and 10).

Fig 9 On a K row, cross main yarn in front of contrasting yarn and drop to back. Knit stitch on left-hand needle using contrasting.

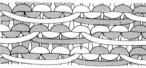

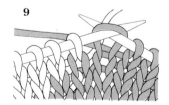

Fig 10 On a P row, pick up contrasting yarn in front of main color and purl next stitch on left-hand needle.

Bobbins. You can make your own bobbins from stiff cardboard. Trace and enlarge the shape given in Fig 11. Draw around enlarged tracing on stiff cardboard, then cut out. Wind

Fig 11 Trace the bobbin shape and cut from stiff cardboard.

sufficient yarn on the bobbin for your color block. Release yarn from the bobbin as you need it (see Fig 12).

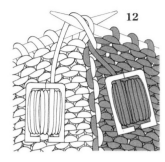

Fig 12 Wind yarns on the bobbins. Do not let them hang too far from your work. Release yarn as required.

12

SEAMING GARMENTS

Backstitch seam. A strong, firm seam which you can use on most garments, although it tends to form a ridge (Fig 13).

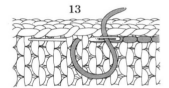

Fig 13 Hold edges together right sides facing. Work back stitches along the seam, 5mm (¹/₄in) from edge of the knitting.

13

Edge-to-edge seam. This seam is more lightweight and is almost invisible if it is properly worked (Fig 14).

Fig 14 Place pieces edge to edge, matching rows and pattern. Sew into the head of opposite stitches alternately.

14

SPECIAL TECHNIQUES

Knitting in the round. In certain situations, such as working a collar, a set of four double-pointed needles is used to make knitting easier (Fig 15).

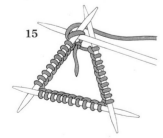

Fig 15 Knitting in the round. Stitches are bind onto three needles, and the fourth is used for working stitches.

15

Duplicate stitch embroidery. Sometimes called Swiss darning, this is a quick and easy method of adding color to garments knitted in stockinette stitch. Fig 16 shows embroidery worked horizontally along the row. Fig 17 shows the technique worked vertically.

Fig 16a When embroidering horizontally, bring needle through at A, insert at B under base of stitch above, bring out at C.

Fig 16b Then insert needle at D and bring through at E ready for next stitch.

16a   16b

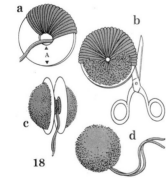

17a   17b

Fig 17a When working vertically, bring needle through at A, insert at B, and bring out at C.

Fig 17b Take the needle under head of stitch below and emerge above it at D, ready for next stitch.

Making pompoms. These can be made to any size and used to trim hats, caps, or mittens.
Cut two cardboard circles 10–13cm (4–5in) diameter. Cut a hole in the center of each. The distance marked "A" in Fig 18a will determine the size of the finished pompom (twice A).
Wind yarn around both circles together until the hole is almost filled (or you can half fill the hole for a less dense pompom). Cut through the yarn between the circles (Fig 18b). Tie a length of yarn between the circles, tear or pull the circles away (Fig 18c). Shake the pompom into shape, trim if necessary (Fig 18d).

Fig 18a Cut two cardboard circles, wind yarn over both circles together.

Fig 18b Cut between circles to release the yarn.

Fig 18c Tie yarn around between cardboard circles to secure the pompom.

Fig 18d Tear or ease the circles off the pompom, trim to shape.

18

Tyrolean flower. The Tyrolean garments on pages 68–75 have flowers embroidered around the bobbles. These are worked in straight stitches and lazy daisy stitches (see Fig 19).

Fig 19 Embroider straight stitches and lazy daisy stitches around the bobble to make a flower effect.

19

List of Retailers

If you have difficulty in obtaining any of the yarns specified in the instructions in this book, contact Rowan Yarns at:

Rowan Yarns
Green Lane Mill
Holmfirth
West Yorkshire
HD7 1RW
Great Britain

Overseas readers please contact:

Australia

Rowan (Australia),
191 Canterbury Road,
Canterbury,
3126 Victoria
Telephone: 03 830 1609

Belgium

Susan Higgin,
Ma Campagne,
rue du village 4,
Septon 5482,
Durbuy
Telephone: 086 213451

Canada

Estelle Designs and Sales Ltd,
38 Continental Place,
Scarborough,
Ontario
Telephone: 416 298 9922

Denmark

Designer Garn,
Aagade 3,
Roerbaek,
DK 9500 Hobro
Telephone: 098 55 7811

Holland

Henk and Henrietta Beukers,
Dorpsstraat 9,
5327 AR Hurwenen
Telephone: 04182 1764

Italy

La Compagnia del Cotone,
Via Mazzini 44,
10123 Torino
Telephone: 011 878381

Japan

Diakeito Co. Ltd,
1-5-23 Nakatsu Kita-Ku
Osaka 531
Telephone: 06 371 5657

Mexico

Rebecca Pick
Estambres Finos y Tejidos
   Finos S.A. de C.V.,
San Francisco 352,
Depto 202,
C.P. 03100,
Colonia del Valle,
Mexico 12 D.F.
Telephone: 05 543 20 35

New Zealand

Creative Fashion Center,
PO Box 45083,
Epuni Railway,
Lower Hutt
Telephone: 04 674 085

Norway

Eureka,
PO Box 357,
1401 Ski
Telephone: 09 871909

Singapore

Classical Hobby House,
1 Jln Anak Bukit,
No. B2-15 Bukit Timah Plaza,
Singapore 2158
Telephone: 4662179

Sweden

Eve Wincent Gelinder,
Wincent, Luntmakargatan 56,
56 113 58 Stockholm
Telephone: 08 32 70 60

United States

Westminster Trading Corporation,
5 Northern Boulevard,
Amherst, New Hampshire 03031
Telephone: (603) 886 5041

West Germany

Textilwerkstatt – Friedenstrasse 5,
3000 Hanover 1
Telephone: 0511 818001